# THE FOUR-MINUTE MILE

# THE FOUR-MINUTE MILE

## Roger Bannister

Guilford, Connecticut
An imprint of The Globe Pequot Press

*To my wife, Moyra, and our children,*
*Erin, Clive, Thurstan, and Charlotte*

The Introduction to the 1981 edition originally appeared in slightly different form in *Sports Illustrated*.

**Library of Congress Cataloging-in-Publication Data**

Bannister, Roger.
  The four-minute mile.

  1. Bannister, Roger. 2. Runners (Sports)—Great Britain—Biography. I. Title.
GV1061.15.B37A3 1989      796.4'26 [B]                    88-37267
ISBN 1-55821-027-X

Manufactured in the United States of America
First edition/Fifth printing

# CONTENTS

# INTRODUCTION
# TO THE 1994 EDITION

1994 marks the fortieth anniversary of the first four-minute mile. The world record now stands at 3 minutes 44.9 seconds in the name of Noureddine Morceli of Algeria. At what point will record-breaking for the mile end? Clearly there is a limit determined by the structure of the human body. In 1981, when I wrote the introduction to the last American edition of this book, I predicted that a 3:30 mile "is not impossible provided some harmony prevails in our uneasy world and the sheer stupidity of political chicanery is held at bay." I still hold firmly to this view.

It is strange that the intrinsically simple and unimportant act of placing one foot after another for 1,760 yards, as fast as possible, should become such an important sporting achievement. I think the appeal lies in its simplicity—it needs no money, no equipment, no particular physique, no knowledge, no education—and in a world of increasingly complex technology, it stands out as a naive statement about the nature of man. A man can, with his own two feet, overcome severe difficulties to reach a pinnacle upon which he can declare 'no one has ever done this before.' The word *challenge* is overused but such acts have a profound reality, especially to the young.

In the past ten years, as in the previous 30, the record has fallen on average by about 0.3 seconds per year. At this rate, the 3:30 mile might be run in the year 2044— 50 years.

Why has there been such steady improvement? One reason is the change from the rough cinder tracks, made from the ash of coal-fired power stations, which were sticky and collected on the long steel-spiked shoes we wore, slowing us down. In the 1960s, fast synthetic tracks gave an advantage of perhaps a second per lap in the mile. Running shoes were also improved when short studs, which caused little resistance in contacting the track, replaced spikes.

But the main reason for the steady improvement lies in the training—more than two hours each day, often in two sessions, instead of my daily 30 minutes! Such intense training is hard to maintain, with threats of commercialism and other distractions constantly lurking. Too many races can exhaust even the strongest athlete and, in some instances, bring on unusual infections, suggesting that very hard training can impair the immune system. Despite the risks, hard training seems necessary if the modern miler is to compete often and to win prize money and pursue what has become a professional career. Sebastian Coe of Britain at one time suffered from the rare infection toxoplasmosis but recovered to set a world record for the mile in 1981 (3:47.30). His showing in the 800 meters in 1981 (1:41.73), is the longest standing world record for middle-distance running. In the Olympic Games of 1980, held in Moscow, he competed in the heats, semi-finals, and finals of the 800 m, and in the heats and finals of the 1,500 m, winning the 1,500 m Gold Medal.

One last factor in the mile world record that must be mentioned is more effective scanning for talented young athletes. Great athletes are likely to occur in proportion to the size of the population—given adequate nutrition, health, training facilities, and incentives are provided. However, political factors can influence a situation and disrupt an athlete's career.

Relatively few major track events have been disrupted by politics, although the United States boycotted the Moscow Olympics and the Soviet Union returned the favor by ignoring the Los Angeles Olympics in 1984. When the Berlin Wall fell and the Soviet Union fell apart, some highly skilled coaches from Eastern Europe were unemployed and offered their skills to other countries, particularly China. In 1993, Chinese women athletes in their late teens set several new world records in middle-distance running. The records were so remarkable that rumors of anabolic steroid use were voiced by several competing countries, and stoutly denied by the Chinese coaches. Chinese men are likely to follow suit. The propoganda value of athletic success is immense now that

China wants to rejoin the world scene after years of Cultural Revolution and self-imposed isolation, but the Chinese must convince the drug-testing authorities and the world that their athletes are drug free.

The four-minute mile is sometimes compared with other athletic achievements of the 1950s which, like the four-minute mile, were thought by some to be impossible. In 1953, Edmund Hilary and Sherpa Tensing climbed Mount Everest. To date, Everest has been climbed by hundreds of people, sometimes without the help of oxygen, and, on one day in 1992, by 30 men and two women. Another feat was the circumnavigation of the world by the single-handed sailor, Francis Chichester, who was in his 60s and commented, "Challenge makes life more intense." Age is less a factor in sailing than in running, but both demand special skills, courage, and endurance.

In the past 40 years, the sub-four-minute mile has been frequently bettered but is still hardly a commonplace occurrence. No man over 40 has achieved it and no woman has come within 10 seconds of it. While I am still around, I look on my successors with hope, wishing them the same enjoyment in running that I experienced during my ten-year career as an athlete so many years ago. I hope something in this book, written when I was 25, might both inspire the serious athlete and yet convey the great joy in running to everyone.

—Sir Roger Bannister
March, 1994

# INTRODUCTION TO THE 1981 EDITION

Why did we ever try to break the four-minute-mile barrier in 1954? Fifty-eight years had passed since the revival of the Olympic Games in 1896, and athletes had been edging toward this goal, the simple act of putting one foot after another faster than anyone had done before. Partly it was the time we lived in; the 1950s were an age of exploration and attempts to smash physical barriers in a world liberated from war, a world in which we were no longer soldiers, bombed, or rationed. My first unsuccessful world-record bid was in 1953, the year Queen Elizabeth II was crowned and the year Everest was scaled. But the world was not yet navigated by a single-handed nonstop sailor and the moon landing was only dreamed of.

Chris Brasher, Chris Chataway, and I, all of us at Oxford University, seemed more privileged than we actually were. We were labeled young "Elizabethans," possessing more than a touch of single-mindedness, op-

1

timism, and that now unfashionable quality, patriotism. Breaking world athletic records offered us an opportunity for intensely personal achievement. Pindar, the Greek poet, captured this idea when he wrote in 500 B.C., "Yet that man is happy and poets sing of him who conquers with hand and swift foot and strength."

After the four-minute mile, I ran almost daily for the next twenty years, but I never competed again. Astonishment at that decision would have been quickly allayed if the questioner had glimpsed my life. As an intern at St. Mary's Hospital in London, I looked after some fifty "beds," a round-the-clock schedule which allowed only a few snatched hours of sleep. It was a punishing (and since much-revised) make-or-break initiation to a teaching-hospital training for a consultant physician, but also an enormously rich and enthralling experience. Medicine, and neurology in particular—the teasing, endless puzzle of how the brain controls our every thought and activity —has captivated me to this day.

Since 1954, there has been a revolution in athletic training. Instead of working out for half an hour five days a week, athletes now run for up to three hours a day over two sessions. As a result of this longer, harder training and faster synthetic tracks, the world mile record has been lowered by several great athletes, whom I have enjoyed meeting and watching in action. Herb Elliott of Australia took the largest slice from the record, lowering it by 2.7 seconds, to 3:54.5 in 1958. Peter Snell of New Zealand was probably a stronger miler than Elliott and he brought

2

the record to 3:54.1 in 1964. But I rate Jim Ryun of the United States as the most talented natural runner, though he was not the best competitor. Ryun was only nineteen when he ran 3:51.3. The achievement of this record was partially due to altitude training, a technique which athletes stumbled upon when faced with the prospect of the 1968 Mexico City Olympics, to be held in the thin air at seventy-five hundred feet. In 1967 Ryun went to a training camp at seventy-four hundred feet. Then twice within six weeks he raced at sea level and lowered world records on each occasion. Unfortunately, this preparation was to no avail in the Olympics, and it was a sad sight when Ryun was beaten in the final, altitude having wrecked any predictability of performance.

Filbert Bayi of Tanzania brought the record down to 3:51 in 1975. He illustrates a second factor responsible for distance record breaking: the advantage of dwelling at high altitudes. Even while one sleeps, the body is training to transport oxygen efficiently from the thin air to the muscles.

Like Snell, John Walker, another great miler of the past two decades, comes from New Zealand, which has a healthy antipodean Anglo-Saxon tradition of sport. He brought the record below 3:50 (3:49.4) in 1975, but his Montreal Olympic gold medal in the fifteen hundred was somewhat devalued by Bayi's withdrawal from the race, robbed of his chance by African politicians using their athletes as pawns in the political battle against apartheid.

3

Just when we were beginning to believe that progress would come only from runners with massive physiques like that of Cuba's Alberto Juantorena, two slightly built British runners, Sebastian Coe and Steve Ovett, set new mile world records in 1979 and 1980, respectively. The apparent ease with which both ran is a promise of still more records to come. (The women's mile record was broken in 1980 by Mary Decker of the United States—she ran it in 4 minutes 21.7 seconds.) With nearly a thousand million Chinese and more than six hundred million Indians waiting in the wings and about to enter the world sports stage, I foresee a continuous and steady progress in athletic record breaking. A 3:30 mile by the turn of the century is not impossible, provided some harmony still prevails in our uneasy world and that the sheer stupidity of political chicanery is held at bay.

Sport at its best means striving for excellence, international cooperation, and an inventive technical genius in elevating further what is, in essence, play within complex rules. But there is a darker, less promising side. Progress that brings the use of medical science to aid the injured athlete or advise the marathon runner on diet and training also brings knowledge of drugs that extend unfairly and dangerously the limits of performance, like evils released from a Pandora's box. The battle against drugs is not a short, sharp skirmish, but will be a long, drawn-out campaign. It needs continuing administrative and pharmacological resources to introduce on a world

4

scale even more sophisticated tests against the few pharmacologists and doctors who are prepared to prostitute their knowledge to gain illegal advantage for their teams. The price of eternal vigilance in sport is going to be high indeed in the next decade.

I am always bombarded with questions about amateurism. The International Olympic Committee (IOC), since Avery Brundage's retirement, has changed its position on amateurism and now permits almost any broken-time financial compensation the international governing bodies approve as reasonable. This applies in Western democracies as well as in socialist Eastern states. I do not quarrel with any of this. Of course it is fairer than the old-fashioned system. But the ability to pay what amounts to a living wage to athletes depends on the economic wealth of the country and the importance it attaches to sporting success and prestige. At present, a promising Third World athlete who wants to participate in sport full time might as well whistle in the wind unless other abilities lead to teaching physical education. Financial compensation is a step toward the goal of equality of opportunity for all to take part in sport, and a reduction in the double-dealing into which athletes have been unwillingly drawn, but it would be healthy if a certain code of moderation could be hammered out. My blood freezes at the thought of athletics becoming one frenetic big-money deal as corrupting for the player as the onlooker. And I must add a warning: Time and again I have noticed that a runner who forsook a part-time job to spend every waking hour on sport was rewarded by a marked deterioration of performance caused by hypochondria and staleness. It may be that some stimulus is necessary to counterbalance the concentration on physical perfection. In 1979 Sebastian Coe broke his world records just after an enforced absence from training due to illness and exams.

More disturbing than the passing of amateurism are the dangers of the increasing size of international events such as the Olympics. This brings commercial exploitation (whose running shoes are worn on the rostrum?) and the abuse by pressure groups seeking a platform with a ready-made television audience of hundreds of millions. I shall never forget the anguish of Munich, with eleven Israelis slain by Palestinian gunmen and Avery Brundage deciding, rightly in my view, that despite all, the Games should continue.

Sport is now too important commercially to be isolated from the world of political events. Though the tradition of suspending hostilities during the Olympics began in ancient Greece, it has been a principle more honored in the breach than the observance. I have some sympathy with African countries demonstrating the strength of their feelings against apartheid with one of their few weapons, but it is certain that such boycotts also damage African countries by denying the world the chance to see the brilliance of their athletes. Taking part might result in greater sympathy for their cause instead of the irritation occasioned by last-minute withdrawals. A further consideration is the bitterness of the athletes themselves when boycotts occur.

Despite the problems that threaten the Games, I remain an enthusiastic and hopeful Olympian, though the content and situs of the Games may need drastic changes. My participation in the Helsinki Olympics in 1952 was a high point of my career—even though I finished in fourth place. The six Olympic Games I have attended and watched since then have left me with memories of pathos and drama far above the petty ordinariness of so much of life.

In all the avalanche of criticism of international sport, it is often forgotten that every athlete who participates becomes a bulwark back in his own country against accepting complete lies about another nation. Once you have competed on the track and queued for food and joked in the shower room you can no longer be persuaded that a foreigner has two horns and a forked tail. In this sense, sporting exchanges are a great hope for the world, and it is in the deepest interest of the world for them to continue.

The revolution that has taken place in top-level sport in the last twenty years has been mirrored by another dramatic change. In the early sixties the British Sports Council examined ways of getting people to take part in sport. Sports facilities in Western democracies have always been the Cinderella of public spending and have been left to local clubs, often sadly impoverished. In

Britain it was hardly surprising that there were so few aspiring athletes, with only half a dozen adequate running tracks in existence and sixty percent of the swimming pools, having been built in Victorian times, linked with the idea of cleanliness rather than healthy recreation. Almost all our schools had fine facilities and compulsory games. So just why did adult participation wither away to a feeble ten percent? Great urban conglomerations and our changeable climate often made the use of playing fields unattractive, but sociological research showed that the vast majority of people yearned to use their leisure more actively. We promoted the indoor sports center—a multipurpose building able to cater to twenty-two sports and often including a swimming pool. Simple restaurants, stage facilities, and nurseries filled out the picture, making our council's rallying cry of "Sport for All" a reality. The moment one town opened a center and people flocked in, neighboring mayors and city governments vied with each other to open similar sporting halls. During my tenure as chairman we saw the number leap from twenty to four hundred. We tried to persuade the larger schools to share their sports facilities with the public in the evenings and on school holidays. Where this happened there was an encouraging drop in the statistics for vandalism and petty crime because it proved such a boon to youngsters cooped up in cities.

Doctors, perhaps, have become too negative, saying no to food, smoking, and alcohol. Now is the time to say a massive yes to positive health. The message now is jogging not tranquilizers, tennis not heart attacks, sports clubs with friends instead of a psychotherapy group. I have always been reluctant to dragoon people into boring fitness routines; I have wanted them to choose activities they find exciting. The heartwarming spontaneity with which Americans grip a good new idea and put it into practice should be a lesson to the rest of the world. Even at noncompetitive levels, running, or jogging, has swept America, becoming the only healthful addiction I know. It now attracts some twenty million Americans who not only feel better, but will also probably live longer. Doubtless there are jogging bores and some other fashion may in time supplant recreational running, but nothing can detract from this remarkable revolution in approach to physical activity. Stemming at first from fear of coronary heart disease, it is now mainly sustained—and this is the important fact—because it is enjoyable for its own sake. Though an ankle injury in 1975 stopped my daily running, I ride my bicycle and still enjoy the sense of muscles used and happily tired, the sense of lungs stretched and a heart that is reaching down for some of its reserves.

There is no doubt that "Sport for All" is a twentieth-century movement of real significance. Other mass movements have oppressed where they intended to liberate. This movement liberates because it has an essential individual basis. The choice of speed, route, distance, or company is entirely yours. Instead of running,

9

you may prefer knocking an innocent ball with a piece of wood or metal or gut. Whatever the choice, it rests in freedom, echoing passions and needs that have primitive evolutionary significance and which to our peril we have too often dismissed as uncivilized and immature. The experience of the past twenty-five years has only served to reinforce my belief in the courage and infinite resourcefulness of athletes the world over. This augurs well for the future.

I hope this book may help others to liberate through running a source of power and excitement within themselves, and even stimulate the sedentary! As a neurologist, I now understand more about such sources of pleasure and pain and the strange, some say mystical, experiences that come to those who extend their physical powers to the limit—and beyond. But science and medicine cannot yet explain why struggles give us deep satisfaction, perhaps the most real satisfaction we ever have in life. With our increasing knowledge of brain chemistry and endorphins I feel confident that in the next ten years we shall come much closer to understanding this paradox.

R. B.

# CHAPTER ONE

# INTRODUCTION

*"Write the vision and make it plain upon tables, that he may run that readeth it."*
BOOK OF HABAKKUK.

WHAT ARE THE MOMENTS that stand out clearly when we look back on childhood and youth?

I remember a moment when I stood barefoot on firm dry sand by the sea. The air had a special quality as if it had a life of its own. The sound of breakers on the shore shut out all others. I looked up at the clouds, like great white-sailed galleons, chasing proudly inland. I looked down at the regular ripples on the sand, and could not absorb so much beauty. I was taken aback—each of the myriad particles of sand was perfect in its way. I looked more closely, hoping perhaps that my eyes might detect some flaw. But for once there was nothing to detract from all this beauty.

In this supreme moment I leapt in sheer joy. I was startled, and frightened, by the tremendous excitement that so few steps could create. I glanced round uneasily to see if anyone was watching. A few more steps—self-consciously now and firmly gripping the original excitement. The earth seemed almost to move with me. I was running now, and a fresh rhythm entered my body. No longer conscious of my movement I discovered a new unity with nature. I had found a new source of power and beauty, a source I never dreamt existed.

From intense moments like this, love of running can grow. This attempt at explanation is of course inadequate, just like any analysis of the things we enjoy—like the description of a rose to someone who has never seen one.

The scientist may attempt an objective explanation. The sense of exercise is an extra sense or perhaps a subtle combination of the others. It is one which most of us ignore. Small electrical impulses, so the scientist tells us, pass from our contracting muscles and our moving joints to our brain. The electrical rhythm produced there is a source of pleasure. Like that caused by music, it has some interplay with the rhythms inherent in our nervous systems. But no explanation is satisfying that does not take account of feelings of beauty or power.

The satisfaction we derive from games is complex. We enjoy struggling to get the best out of ourselves, whether we play games of skill requiring quickness of eye and deftness of touch, or games of effort and endurance like athletics. It is not just the desire to succeed. There is the need to feel that our bodies have a skill and energy of their own, apart from the man-made machines they may drive. There is the desire to find in sport a companionship with kindred people. I have found all these.

12

The sportsman enjoys his sport even if he has absolutely no prospect of becoming a champion. In athletics there are many events, running, jumping, and throwing, which suit different physiques, the long and thin, the broad and strong. Industry and perseverance, without any great natural aptitude, bring greater success in athletics than is possible in ball games.

For nearly ten years I have been running many times a week and my grasp of the reasons why I run continues to grow. Running through mud and rain is never boring. Like 100,000 cross-country runners, their number ever increasing, I find in running—win or lose—a deep satisfaction that I cannot express in any other way. However strenuous our work, sport brings more pleasure than some easier relaxation. It brings a joy, freedom and challenge which cannot be found elsewhere.

Does this primitive joy remain when I put on shoes with three-quarter inch steel spikes and run round a circular cinder track, only to come back to the starting point? What is it like to have the excitement of competitive struggle grafted on the natural freedom found in movement—to champion the cause of club or country and to have their honour, as well as your own, at stake? What difference does it make when the sound of breakers on the shore is replaced by the roar of a crowd of 50,000 spectators in a stadium, crying out for more and more effort and identifying themselves with each runner's success or failure? What does it mean to wait

13

weeks or months for a race which only lasts for a few minutes—to travel thousands of miles for the few seconds of supreme exertion before reaching the winning post?

Until quite recently, if I had been asked what running meant to me I should have replied "I don't know." Life must be lived forwards even if sometimes it only makes sense as we look back. Before now it would have been impossible for me to attempt to write about running, but now I can see a pattern of striving—of success and failure—which I hope will grow clearer. Though I have only experience of my own running, this story, I feel, applies to athletics in general, to other sports, and I hope even beyond. That is my justification for overcoming a reticence which makes me shrink from writing about my own feelings. This description may be helpful to others who may have experienced these same emotions but are not prepared to talk, let alone write, about them. I must try to steer a course between false modesty on the one hand and conceit on the other. I shall write mainly as though running were all important. It will be difficult to describe how moments when running seems utterly insignificant alternate with moments when it threatens to engulf me.

In the next chapter there is a picture of the last important race in which I competed—the European Championships in Berne in the summer of 1954. This race is described first, because it contrasts the complexity of

14

such a struggle with the simplicity of my first impulse to run.

In the rest of the book I attempt to trace the way my primitive desire to run brought me into the competitive atmosphere of big races.

# CHAPTER TWO

# EUROPEAN GAMES

## BERNE 1954

*"And thick and fast they came at last
And more and more and more."*
THROUGH THE LOOKING GLASS.

THE POLITICAL FERMENT in Europe seemed to have transferred itself to the Berne Stadium. The 29th of August was a sweltering cloudless day, and 30,000 people sat cheering, chanting and waving flags. Switzerland, as in politics, was neutral in the struggle. Her few competitors were forgotten in the confused impact of blond Scandinavians, swarthy Southerners, burly iron men from the East, and pale Englishmen from the West. At times it seemed as though the strong winds of encouragement and hope from compatriots blew in from each corner of the Stadium, creating a whirlwind in the centre that blew the competitors faster and faster round the track.

It was the last day of the European Championships of 1954. These quadrennial Games are the most important event in world athletics during the four years between the Olympic Games. The winners gain the awards most coveted of all, ranking only below the Olympic titles.

16

I was competing in the next furious struggle, the 1,500 metres. I knew what to expect—a well-meaning mêlée of arms and legs. It was the sort of race in which anything could happen. I felt it was a spectacle more than a fair athletic competition; but that is the way sportsmen on the Continent seem to like their running—a contact sport, too intimate for my liking. It was in just such a race, the Olympic Final of 1952 at Helsinki, that I had come fourth and been dubbed "a failure." This was attributed by many newspapers at the time to my unsuitable training methods—a criticism to which my only answer was silence until the next big race gave me the chance to prove my ideas were right.

This was my second chance. But this time there had been only one day of heats (eliminating races) instead of two, as in the Olympics, and there had been two days interval before the Final. Despite a series of outstanding performances by the British team, many of whom had excelled themselves, Britain was still without a gold medal in the men's events. Little Hungary—someone reminded us—had already won three. In the words of the Olympic dictum we were "fighting well" but not "conquering." How many worlds between a gold medal and second place!

I could not see myself in the winning place. But as at Helsinki mine was the unenviable position of being expected to win.

In some ways, the heat on the previous Thursday was as great an ordeal as the Final. The thought suddenly

17

came—how awful to be knocked out and left to watch the Final from the stands! And the little things that can go wrong! I was warming up on the uneven grass near the track, like a racehorse in the paddock, under the curious eyes of those who could not afford to buy tickets or who were only interested as autograph hunters. I suddenly noticed that my best pair of spikes had split along the side—trivial perhaps, but most unsettling. I had to wear another pair with spikes which were too long, increasing the danger of tripping up. I was not mentally prepared for the heat, and as a result took fright at the last minute when I found myself surrounded by aggressive looking athletes from other countries. The one next to me had been involved on a previous occasion in a skirmish with a British athlete, first on the track and then off it. He still carried a fierce look in his eye. I smiled sweetly at him as if to say, "You and I are good friends," very much the sickly smile that Charlie Chaplin reserved in his early films for policemen and heavyweight champions. This time there was no skirmish, but I caught his elbow at the first bend.

I ran extremely badly, like a startled rabbit, darting up and down amongst the runners in an unnecessarily agitated way. Looking back now it seems a nightmare, but I qualified for the Final in third position, in the relatively easy time of 3 min. 51.8 sec.

In the two days following the heat I had been preparing myself for the Final. I went away for long walks, seeking the mental calm I needed. By Sunday when the

Final came I had built myself up to withstand any set-back. I no longer wanted to be wrapped in cotton wool. If my spikes had split now I should have run in bare feet. If I were knocked over I should not feel martyred, but would draw new impetus from my anger.

With military precision we walked out on the track in the order of our starting position, like prisoners in Indian file. Each one of us perhaps was listening for the calls from his countrymen that told him he was not alone. At this time in particular it was a great encourage-ment that Ian Boyd, one of the younger members of the British team, had reached the Final and was running with me. I very much admired his outward calm, which concealed great strength and tenacity, and gave me the companionship I needed.

There were only eleven lining up for the start. The twelfth man, Langenus of Belgium, had not recovered from a foot injury received while running in my heat. My great disappointment was that one runner was not there—Jose Barthel, reigning Olympic champion—who had not qualified to represent his country. I had been looking forward to getting my revenge for Helsinki. Re-venge is really too strong a word because Barthel was a great Olympic champion, and I was happy that he won so deservedly. But nothing is cancelled out in running—I wanted a complete victory, and it would not be com-plete if he were not running.

To come now to some of the others. Iharos of Hungary was favourite on the basis of times, but was otherwise an unknown quantity. He had helped Hungary on two occasions to capture the 4 × 1,500 metres relay World record. A few weeks before the Games he had in a single race defeated the Norwegian Boysen, broken Gunder Haegg's world record for 1,500 metres, and run the fastest lap recorded in a race of that speed. Of him there were rumours of sleepless nights and great anxiety. He looked thin, angular, and excitable like a thoroughbred.

All the others had done sufficient racing for me to have some idea of their capabilities. Gunnar Nielsen (Denmark) was by far the best "fighter" in the field, and had reached fourth place in the Olympic 800 metres at Helsinki in 1952. In 1954 he had on three occasions run over two seconds faster than my best time for 800 metres. Nielsen was tall and sandy-haired, a natural runner, well versed in the jostle of continental running. He and Audun Boysen, a good friend of his from Norway, had decided to run in different races, Boysen having chosen the 800 metres. This had disappointed me, because Boysen would certainly have set a pace which might well have resulted in a new world record in our race. Instead, the race might become a procession because no one would take the lead.

Next there was Werner Lueg, a Berlin schoolmaster, who had equalled the world record for the 1,500 metres a few weeks before Helsinki, and thereby become Olympic favourite. He was a clever tactician and very confident. He was liberal in good advice to other competitors

—telling me, as we sat waiting on a bench in the centre of the track, not to put on my spikes too soon. Then there was Stanislav Jungwirth, the cheerful Czech, who had beaten me soundly over 880 yards at Whitsun, after my strange "goodwill" visit to New York. He was a powerful runner but inclined to be inconsistent.

Finally came Denis Johansson, the chain-smoking Finn, who had tremendous natural ability but might have sapped some of this by too much running in America. There were five other runners, any one of whom might come through to win, after the giants had battled each other to a standstill. In the light of what happened later, I recall now a letter written home before the race in which I singled out Nielsen as the runner I feared most.

We lined up behind the starting post—eleven anxious athletes, a colourful sight in our national vests, if one had time for such thoughts. "Auf die plätze"—"Get to your marks"; "Fertig"—"Set." We crouched forward expectantly—the gun fired. One runner was too eager and anticipated it. As always I was a little slower off the mark than the rest. I could not help smiling; it seemed so unnecessary to beat the gun in a race that would last for 3¾ minutes. We crouched again—this time we were off.

The starting line is curved, so that each runner shall cover approximately the same distance. We all accelerated in line, inevitably converging—the outside men moving inwards to get good positions, the inside men

21

forced to run straight. I was a little behind the main line, and 15 yards from the start they all crashed into each other. Mugosa of Jugoslavia fell, and only by jumping over him did I avoid transfixing his hand with my spiked running shoe. I might just as easily have been the one to fall. The leaders tore round the first bend in a bunch, three abreast. I was last. No one wanted to lead, yet no one was content to be last—except me.

Soon the leading runner slowed down, worried at being unable to see what was happening behind him. The runner at his shoulder, hustled by a discontented rearguard, was forced into the lead himself. The race was slowing down. The half mile was 4 seconds below four-minute-mile standard. I rested in eighth position from the jostling elbow work to glance up at the enormous clock at the end of the Stadium, with its ruthless second-hand recording our progress round the track. I knew it was dangerous to look up, because for a moment I was unguarded against the man outside me who was cutting in, the man behind who was pushing me, and the man in front whom I might well trip over. None of this jostling is deliberate, of course; it is just that eleven men are running at the top speed within their compass, and no difference between them will show until the last 300 yards of the race.

Each runner worries the others. The anxiety of being pressed and jostled increases; soon it will become too much for someone and he will make an effort to break away from the field. It is this controlled tension about

22

to break down that gives miling its great excitement for the spectators. The early cheering of the crowd was now stilled, and the expectant hush had a positive quality that linked every spectator with the runners on the track. It was certain to be one of the favourites who would try to break away first. Which was it to be—Jungwirth, Lueg, Iharos, Nielsen or myself?

The decision to "break away" results from a mixture of confidence and lack of it. The "breaker" is confident to the extent that he suddenly decides the speed has become slower than he can himself sustain to the finish. Hence he can accelerate suddenly and maintain his new speed to the tape. But he also lacks confidence, feeling that unless he makes a move now, everyone else will do so and he will be left standing. The spurt is extremely wasteful because it is achieved at the cost of relaxation, which should be maintained throughout the race. The athlete's style and mood change completely when he accelerates. His mind suddenly starts driving an unwilling body which only obeys under the stimulus of the excitement. The earlier in the race this extra energy is thrown in, the greater the lead captured, but the less the chance of holding it. The surprise of being first to break away is worth an immediate advantage of 20 yards when there remains one further lap to complete (with a high danger of being overtaken before the finish), an advantage of 10 yards if half way round the last lap, or of 5 yards in the final straight. The "break" is like suddenly exposing your hand in a game of cards. You show how much re-

23

serve you have left by the speed at which you try to open up a gap, and by the point at which you start to do so.

If Landy had been in the race he would have been the first to break—or he would have led all the way. I knew Denmark's Gunnar Nielsen was bound to leave his finish as late as possible. Since he was easily the fastest half-miler in the field it would suit him best to make the race into a dawdle, ending with a fast finish, in which his speed would tell. I guessed that Jungwirth the Czech, very nervous and not so sure of his finish, would "break" first. The German Lueg, with the knowledge that he had shot his bolt too soon in the Olympic Final, might be the second man to try to break away. Iharos from Hungary was still an unknown quantity. I could not see him when I looked around the field at the bell, which is rung when the runners have only one more lap to go. I moved out into the second lane so that I could manœuvre more easily and avoid the danger of being boxed in.

The background noise from the crowd began to rise again. I moved up to Jungwirth's shoulder. He was eager to shoot off and only waiting for a stimulus. The mere presence of another runner outside him was sufficient. The crowd roared as he gained a lead of a yard or so, but the rest of us were soon up to him again. I kept at his shoulder as we rounded the next bend and entered the long back straight before the finish.

I had decided that the place where I could make the most of my finishing burst was 220 yards from the tape, and so I wanted to hold Lueg and the others back until this point—just before the last bend. If I started sprinting earlier, Iharos or an outsider might catch me on the finishing post as I tired. If I started later, Nielsen might outsprint me. I kept at Jungwirth's shoulder, forcing him to keep up a good pace if he was to retain the lead. I felt in command until suddenly I sensed someone closing up on my own shoulder and about to move past me. It was Nielsen, as I learnt later.

We were nearly at the last bend now. I waited anxiously for two or three more strides, almost sandwiched between Jungwirth and Nielsen. If I allowed anyone to overtake me now I should have to satisfy myself with third position until the finishing straight. Alternatively, if I overtook the second runner, the first would be able to make me run wide round the bend and waste precious energy in covering extra distance. The longer I could hold off those behind me the better, because Jungwirth's speed was a good stride for me, and all the time I was building up a reserve of energy preparatory to sprinting. But so were the others.

We reached the bend. Jungwirth, I hoped, imagined himself securely in the lead until the home straight. As the bend began I struck past him with all my power, feeling like an engine with the supercharger full on. I gained valuable yards before Nielsen realised what had happened. I later discovered he came up to me at the beginning of the straight, but I drew away to win by 5 yards. This was probably not more than the distance

25

I gained through the surprise of the sudden acceleration. Never did my finishing burst serve me so well. There was no longer any need to call on emotion to produce this ability to take an over-draft on my energy. There had been times in other races when I felt real fear as I tore down the finishing straight as if my life depended on it—such were the temper and distortion of values produced by my excitement during a race.

This time it was different—I was calm. Just as I had not spent the previous night bathed in sweat, racing the distance a dozen times in my imagination, so it was in the race itself. My mind remained quite cool and detached. It merely switched over the lever, and well-worn channels carried to my body the extra energy that my mind unleashed. As I came down the finishing straight I was moving with all the speed I could possibly have mustered even if I had been running for my life (25 seconds for the last 220 yards). I remember coolly looking up at the clock and thinking: "What a pity! No world record today—the final time will be about 3.44—if only Boysen had been with us!" The race was run in 3 min. 43.8 sec., a championship record and 1.4 seconds (10 yards) faster than the 1952 Olympic Final, a race of the same jostling kind.

The crowd had their spectacle. But I feel strongly that there should be a maximum of eight, not twelve, runners in a race of this kind. This would give the competitors the best possible chance of running instead of scrambling. The spectators would still have their

26

thrill, and for those who are stop-watch minded the time would be faster. The final placings were:

|  |  | Min. | Sec. |
|---|---|---|---|
| 1. R. G. Bannister .. .. | .. | 3 | 43.8 |
| 2. G. Nielsen (Denmark) .. | .. | 3 | 44.4 |
| 3. S. Jungwirth (Czechoslovakia) | .. | 3 | 45.4 |
| 4. I. Eriksson (Sweden) .. | .. | 3 | 46.2 |
| 5. W. Lueg (Germany) .. | .. | 3 | 46.4 |
| 6. S. Iharos (Hungary) .. | .. | 3 | 47.0 |
| 7. D. Johansson (Finland) .. | .. | 3 | 47.4 |
| 8. G. Dohrow (Germany) .. | .. | 3 | 48.2 |
| 9. I. H. Boyd (Gt. Britain) .. | .. | 3 | 49.2 |
| 10. J. Kakko (Finland) .. .. | .. | 3 | 51.8 |

Mugosa (Jugoslavia) fell, and abandoned the race.

# CHAPTER THREE

# EARLY DAYS

*"With the first dream that comes with the
first sleep, I run, I run."*

ALICE MEYNELL.

IT IS DIFFICULT TO REMEMBER what we thought of things
before we began to grow up—before we were fully conscious of ourselves. As a boy I had no clear understanding of why I wanted to run. I just ran anywhere and
everywhere—never because it was an end in itself, but
because it was easier for me to run than to walk. My
walk was ungainly, as though I had springs in my knees.
I always felt impatient to see or do something new, and
running saved time.

In part my running grew out of an intensity and enthusiasm I have always had. Games and adventures
swallowed me up and swept me along until some setback
would make me give up. Like other children I used to
build models of machines in imitation of things I had
seen. I can remember a great three-wheeler trolley built
out of an old-fashioned wooden draining board. I was
interested most in things that moved—the faster the better. I made up for my lack of knowledge of carpentry
by increased use of nails. "Just a minute," I would say,

"one more nail will fix it." One of my boats was so covered with nails that it nearly sank. Non-plussed, I turned it into a submarine. The only things that I built without nails were model aeroplanes, but few of them flew successfully. Usually I played alone.

As every child does, I wondered what life had in store for me. I can distinctly remember moments when my life seemed clear ahead, free of obstacles I had overcome, though I cannot remember what these obstacles were. Now I wonder whether this was just wishful thinking or a sign of determination to spare no effort of mind or body. If there is ever a time when the real core of a person is revealed it is in childhood. Perhaps we all have some concept of our own "specialness" and purpose at a very early age, but we never dare to admit it.

The first time that called for a practical use of my running was when I had been trespassing on some building land near my home. A school friend shouted from the safe side of the fence that the builder was coming. I shot down from a high tree, reached the fence and vaulted it. It might have been easier to talk my way out of trouble on such occasions, but at the time it was easier to run than to think. I found afterwards that my hands and clothes were torn by barbed wire which I had not noticed in the frenzy of excitement caused by fear.

I wonder how much part sheer fright plays in running. There was a long passage near my home patrolled by a gang of boys bigger and tougher than me. I was about eight at the time, shy, timid and easily frightened. This gang used to capture other boys and hold them in their "den," submitting them, I imagined, to torture, the very thought of which kept me awake at night. The threat "snowballed" in my mind and I would walk miles to avoid this particular passage. One day I was half way through before I thought of the danger. Then I saw the gang in a huddle. At first I tried to go on, keeping my eyes fixed on them. I felt sick with fright as I knew they were waiting for me. My steps grew more leaden, my temples pounded, my body seemed about to burst as I drew closer. I knew I ought to try to walk through, but fright won before I reached them. I turned and ran, with my head tucked down, my arms flailing vigorously. I tore round the first corner, round the second, and down the road to the safety of my own house. Then a sense of shame overtook me. But I had learned the value of fright as an aid to speed.

I ran for it when I heard my first air-raid siren. I was ten and sailing my boat on a pond half a mile from home. At the first terrifying whine I tucked my boat under my arm—war or no war one had to retain a sense of proportion and of property. By the time the moaning crescendo reached its loudest I had taken to my heels. I imagined bombs and machine guns raining on me if I didn't go my fastest. Was this a little of the feeling I have now when I shoot into the lead before the last bend and am afraid of a challenge down the finishing straight? To move into the lead means making an attack requiring fierceness and confidence, but fear must play some part in the last stage, when no relaxation is possible and all discretion is thrown to the winds.

The city of Bath was the background to my first competitive running, my family having moved there at the outbreak of war. The years I spent there are too close for me to be entirely dispassionate about them. One of the very few advantages of writing in my middle twenties is that it is still possible to remember adolescence as a time of both turmoil and frustration. I am too young to be able to smile benignly and say what a thoroughly happy life I had at school. I remember only too well what it was actually like. Perhaps only the young should be allowed to reminisce about childhood, because only they can remember disappointment as well as happiness. They are not old enough to see everything in the distorting mirror of time or dimmed by the haze of forgetfulness.

I was not very strong physically. Until I was about thirteen the week often ended with a nervous headache and an attack of violent sickness. Each day I grew more tense and excitable until the climax at the weekend. Perhaps it was lucky I was at a day school, the City of Bath Boys' School. Every day I climbed the steps cut in Beechen Cliff, overlooking the city. I disliked the feeling of being weighed down by clothes and books, and on the way home I felt like flinging away all burdens.

31

I would leap down the steps three at a time until I reached the bottom exhausted.

I lived very much in a world of my own. Having started in a new school nearly a term late I felt out of step for a while. It was an unusual mixed atmosphere, half the boys being local residents and the rest, like myself, evacuees from London. I was more at home with my own group of boys from London, and even with the masters, than with the local boys. These did not take their lessons so seriously, and we had a sense that they resented us as intruders. They must have thought us priggish and aloof in return.

Things came to a climax for me with a taunt and a challenge from another boy, which involved me in my first major sporting event. He was the class's bruiser, known to take lessons in boxing, which left me at a hopeless disadvantage. Luckily, the fight took place in the gym under official conditions and was stopped before I was damaged too much. I crept home that day not so much hurt by the punishment as by the shame of being beaten. I never told my parents. After this I practised boxing a little with my father, and no doubt dreamt of taking on all comers, but in my heart I knew that my fists were not my real weapons.

I took everything so seriously that there were quite a few upsets, both at school and at home. I found relief in my love of exploration and discovery. On a second-hand bicycle, built when weight was thought to be a virtue, and with defective brakes and a slipping three-speed gear, I scoured the countryside seeking out my own private haunts. A new world of mystery and adventure opened to me. I tried to paint sketches of valleys that I liked, or perhaps to draw a castle I had until then seen only in books. Somerset had a richness and a warmth possessed by no other county I had ever seen. Stone houses sink into the background of trees and hills. There is infinite variety. Bath itself gave me an interest in history. It was so easy to imagine Beau Nash in the Pump Room, Hogarth characters in the Assembly Rooms, and ladies carried in Sedan chairs from their houses in the Royal Crescent. It was even possible to imagine the Romans bathing in the hot springs, and farther afield the ancient Britons near their burial mounds.

This was the background to my first junior cross-country race. It was an annual event, and the whole school turned out, except, I remember, the fat boys who were excused. In my first year, when I was about eleven, I did no training. I went off very fast, with the fixed notion that despite my age I was going to win. The sheer exertion was extremely painful, and I came in about eighteenth, completely exhausted.

Next year my House Captain told me to train. I decided that this time I would win, if only as a challenge to the Bath "onions." My training consisted of running round the 2½ mile course twice a week as fast as I could, then limping off home and taking two days to recover. One result was that I developed pains in my heels, and was told it was my Achilles tendon. This sounded a most professional injury to have so I told my friends about it— "Yes, Achilles tendon trouble, all good runners get it at some time or other."

No one of my age had won the race before, so I did not have to worry about being the favourite. But this did not prevent me from lying awake the night before. I thought hard about tucking my head well down (this was what my gym master advised), and chasing the third form giant who had won the race last year. I had been quietly watching him for some time. He had no idea who I was, of course, and my keen eye detected signs of his over-confidence, and of unfitness through lack of training. I won the race, and remember with pleasure the utter astonishment of all my school friends. I hardly mentioned it to my parents—I was becoming very secretive about all I did.

This victory restored some of my waning self-respect, and I settled down to other activities with renewed vigour. In the peculiar convention of English schools it now seemed that I would be allowed by my school fellows to work hard because I also won races. It was apparently the magic formula for being accepted by those who never worked at all. This was the moment when I stumbled upon the technique of masquerading as the good games-playing schoolboy. This discovery "worked," and gave me greater freedom in the next few years to follow my own inclinations. I blossomed in sidelines as actor, musician, archæologist, and I was very happy.

I worked furiously, because everything interested me and—I must not forget—won the annual junior cross-country race. It wasn't easy to win, but I was conscious of accepting the discomfort as the price of freedom to work, and gain the toleration, if not the respect, of the other boys for the rest of the year. Looking back now the situation seems farcical. I am sure that I was not a better runner than the others, in the sense of having more innate ability. I just knew I had to win for the sake of peace. It was as simple as that.

I always finished in the last stages of exhaustion, but I refused to let anyone beat me. My lungs felt too small for their task. Over the last half mile there was a steep hill, and I used to make an alarming noise like an hysterical girl sobbing as I gasped for breath. It worried people, but I never felt as bad as I looked. The delight of ensuring peace for another year made me forget the discomfort.

In my last year in this race there was a general feeling that it was somehow improper that I should still be a junior, though in the fourth form, but it was settled on age. I had all the misgivings of being favourite, but won the race for the third time. I expected, perhaps with no justification, to be given the cup—an enormous silver one. It amused me to think of the masters digging deeply into their pockets to buy a new one, all because of my happening to run rather fast. Instead of this they gave me a small replica, but it was real silver, and I was immensely proud. At the time it was my most treasured possession and the symbol of my freedom. It is the only cup I remember being allowed to keep, apart from a similar one as junior Victor Ludorum. When I next began collecting sports trophies, cups had gone out of fashion, the nearest equivalent being tankards, which unlike cups, could be used.

In the next two years in Bath I took no interest in organised running—in a way it had served its purpose. My bicycle expeditions grew longer and longer, 70 miles in a day was a common average, and now I often went with school friends.

My concentration on school work caused me to slip up badly on one occasion. Having a slight cold, I left school with a satchel full of books and spent three days at home studying. I returned to school just before some exams for which I now felt very well prepared, only to discover that I had missed an important house match. The rugger team, of which I was a member, had ended a disastrous season with an overwhelming defeat. It appeared that several other members of the team were also missing on the crucial day, though not necessarily studying.

I went to the weekly House Meeting. Without any warning I found myself listening to a charge of cowardice levelled by the Housemaster himself at those who had missed the match. I suddenly realised that this included me. . . . I was aghast. He did not mince words, and talked about rats that desert the sinking ship. I had never felt shame like this before. The fact that my absence had nothing to do with the house match, which I had completely forgotten, did nothing to help. I doubted whether I should be able to raise my head again. I had returned to school happy and confident for my exams, to find myself suddenly faced with this horrible shame. Life took such sudden twists. Even when things were going well there was a feeling of impending disaster. You might always be caught for some offence you thought was undiscovered—or worse still, that you never committed. I stared at my exam paper that morning, dazed and unable to think.

I realised then how delicately one's individual freedom is poised. Though most of us were perhaps unaware of it, the school was in fact governed more by fear in one way or another, than by respect or tolerance. This made compromises difficult either with other boys or with the masters. Under these conditions, freedom to explore and expand was always in danger.

I remember one farewell comment from my first form master. Mr. Guerrier had taken me to his home after my first day at the school when I had travelled from London alone. He smoothed over my first day's nervous tension (I was ten at the time), and so won my unshakable fondness and respect. Ever since he had been telling me to take things easily, and his parting words were, "You'll be dead before you're twenty-one if you go on at this rate."

When I returned to London my confidence left me. I had matriculated in Bath, and went straight into the sixth form of University College School, Hampstead. This is a school with high traditions—not a boarding school, but a day school from the deliberate choice of the founders. Most of the boys had imbibed the school traditions from the first form upwards, and many had passed through a preparatory school of the same foundation. The basis of my own self-respect had never been very secure. Here I was overawed by my new surroundings and my carefully built superstructure collapsed like a house of playing cards. My bewilderment returned and the facade of confidence was gone. I felt a small country fish in a very large London pond.

Nothing else has produced such acute and intense self-consciousness as I suffered then. I thought it was entirely peculiar to myself but realise now it must be a fairly common experience. I became nervous and tongue-tied, blushing violently when anyone spoke to me or tried to overcome my conviction of my own unworthiness. Worst of all, I could not see any way out. The obsession grew until it absorbed the whole energy of my thought. As my respect for everyone and everything at the school increased, so did the sense of my own inadequacy and hence my embarrassment. The vicious circle continued.

38

It is strange how when we pass through a stage like this the boys above us in school and the school itself take on vast dimensions. The boys all seemed grown men except me. I hovered uneasily on the brink, wondering what would become of me. The masters seemed like Members of Parliament, or even Royalty, and the school itself like a vast cathedral, broad and deep as the earth itself.

I was silent and irascible at home, betraying my feelings only indirectly. I was bewildered that life could change so quickly. I hoped I was not really inferior in ability to the majority of the boys at the school, but how could I get control of myself again? Only dimly could I understand the change taking place in me, so I felt angry and impatient. Whatever potentiality there was in me was bottled up inside. Somehow I guessed from my previous experience that sport was the only outlet that could break the deadlock.

It is strange how we strive unwittingly towards our own treatment and cure, battling our heads against many doors until we find one already open. Enlightened as the school was, the boys who wielded authority as prefects were games players and not intellectuals. I re-applied the formula of my earlier way of living in Bath with greater energy than I had shown before. It was disappointing to me that running was not a popular sport at the school, though now I would agree with the Headmaster that rugger is possibly better for boys. I was unsuited to rugby by temperament and physique, being at this time

39

very tall and thin, and entirely devoid of any power or
short burst of speed. All things considered I achieved
a reasonable standard. But it was not enough for my
self-esteem to do anything half well.

After only a year at the school, the Headmaster—I
presume it was he because he arranged most things—
decided to make me Captain of a House. I have never
quite understood why he did this. There were others
who had far better claim according to the sporting quali-
fications on which selection seemed to depend. I could
not refuse, much as I should have liked to. I suppose the
Headmaster thought it might "bring me out," and help
me to regain the confidence which it was so painfully
obvious I had lost. The result was exactly the opposite.
It drove me underground. I felt that there was nothing
in me that the other boys could possibly respect—at any
rate on the standard of schoolboy values, so how could
I be their leader? Clearly I had no command over myself, so how could I command others? Life was just one
big blush.

At this time I remember suddenly recovering my flu-
ency for one brief moment. There was a school debate
and the Headmaster was defending the organisation of
authority in the school. I made my first public speech.
Quivering with emotion I delivered a broadside of elo-
quence that startled me as much as it did everyone else.
It was as if someone was speaking through me. The
speech came from my bottled up emotions, without my
knowing what I was saying. I delivered a violent attack

40

on the method of selecting those in authority because they were good at games. My enthusiasm was sincere, but I realise now that the basis of my indignation was that I was not good at games. It is obvious to me now, and I expect it was transparent to others at the time, that my motives were confused.

I was attacking the system instead of attacking myself. I had now travelled the full circle. Even then I dimly understood, yet because I was so self-centred there seemed no way out. I decided the problem would remain with me until I left the school. I accepted my position as a misfit while I stayed there, though I went on telling myself that things would not necessarily be the same in the outside world.

I devised a plan of action—at all costs I must leave school at the end of the year. I sat for a scholarship exam at Cambridge when I was sixteen. Meanwhile I played games as hard as I could. I felt resigned—what more could I do? Once or twice I ran on Hampstead Heath. Given the choice between a solitary run and a series of meaningless and, for me, difficult exercises in the gym, I always chose the run. The result is that I still cannot touch my toes, but then runners never have to.

During that year I was a member, and at one match, owing to casualties, became the captain of the worst second rugger "XV" the school has ever had. At half time a "cricketing" score had been piled up against us. The referee, a master at our opponents' school, lost his impartiality for a moment and came over to my sorry side. He had a pained look on his face.

"Excuse me," he said. "You are the captain, aren't you? Please do try to pull your team together. I am sure you can do better than this."

It was one of those occasions in life when the earth fails to open under your feet and you just have to go on living as though you do not care. After this I pretended a casual attitude towards games, typified by some such remark as, "after all one has to take exercise," but I did not deceive myself that I really felt sport was unimportant.

In the summer I tried my hand at rowing. I had the feeling that here was a sport in which effort, of which I had plenty, was more important than skill, of which I seemed to have so little. I tried very hard to look both neat and powerful, though in fact I was neither. I got a creeping paralysis in my wrists, through inadequate strength, when we had rowed about half a full course. I also caught more than my quota of crabs, and I felt that this did not pass entirely unnoticed. Gradually I climbed from the third "eight" to an insecure place in the second.

We proved to be a remarkable crew, and on one glorious occasion beat the first "eight." By occasionally sneaking a glance sideways I could see my oars were making some splendid "puddles." They compared very favourably with those made by the boy in front of me, whom I suspected of being lazy. But the coach did not share my views, and next week I found myself relegated to the third "eight." How galling it was, being unable to convince anyone that my absence from the second "eight" was responsible for their resounding defeat next time!

I was offered a place at Cambridge if I would wait a year, but Oxford would take me in the following October. On what slender accidents are our future loyalties decided! This thought was often in my mind in later athletic struggles against Cambridge.

In my last six months at school I took things more calmly, and enjoyed life more. I knew I was leaving school, perhaps in undignified haste, but at any rate before the Headmaster was faced with the invidious task of deciding whether to pass me over for school prefect, and possibly taking my House from me. It all seems so unimportant now.

I am sure that the conflict I experienced then was mainly due to the ordinary difficulties of growing up, which most boys experience in one form or another. We look around for something we can be good at, even if it is only playing the fool, and if we find it, the transitions from boy to man is made much easier.

I joined the school in the sixth form but with the inferiority complex of a boy in the first. The organisation of the school was first class, but this only added to my difficulties. I never recovered from the shock of entering the school so late, and I wonder how many other boys suffered from similar breaks during the war years.

When I asked Robert Morley, the actor, on the B.B.C. "Frankly speaking" programme, whether he enjoyed his days at school, and received a downright "No!", I was glad to see the bubble pricked of "The happiest days of your life."

# CHAPTER FOUR

# OXFORD — INITIATION

*"Now, here, you see, it takes all the running
you can do, to keep in the same place."*
THROUGH THE LOOKING GLASS.

I WENT UP TO OXFORD in the autumn of 1946 to study medicine. For several years I had felt convinced that a doctor's life would satisfy my ideals most completely. I knew, however, that it would be at least six years before I could qualify as a doctor—with the responsibilities this carries. And so while I had no responsibilities I felt I had to look round for some relief from the restrictions of study.

In Oxford, I had been told, a man without a sport is like a ship without a sail. Here, it seemed, you could both work and play, each being complementary to the other. The idea appealed to me, the only question being to decide which sport to take up. It is often a chance that makes a man choose running instead of rowing, boxing instead of rugger. Of all sports, running seemed to me the only one for which I had any aptitude. I eliminated ball games because I just did not have the eye.

Also I was too light to throw my weight about either in a rowing boat or on the rugby field.

But it was much more than a negative decision to take up serious running. For one thing my sense of frustration, after playing games that did not suit me, had left me with the desire to outstrip my fellows at something— as we all want to do—and the running track seemed the only place left.

Much more important was that since 1945, when I watched my first international athletic meeting, I had a schoolboy dream of becoming a runner. I had never watched anything more than school sports until my father took me to the White City. Perhaps he wanted me to be a runner. He himself had won his school mile and promptly fainted afterwards—as so many runners did in those days. My father and I turned into the road that leads to the Stadium and saw it packed with an impatient crowd, milling about and trying to get inside. This was the first international meeting since the war—and after six years of fighting everyone turned with relief to sport for the satisfaction of competitive struggle.

Before we reached the gates they were closed—there were already fifty thousand people inside. The crowd in front was determined to surge its way in. Someone pushed over a barrier, a police cordon broke, and before I recovered my breath I was inside the coveted ground, happy to stand for four hours.

The main feature of the meeting was that Sydney Wooderson was challenging Arne Andersson, the great Swedish runner. After several years of competition in Sweden during war time, Andersson had led Gunder Haegg up to the last bend, and forced him to set up a new world record for the mile of 4 min. 1.4 sec., a time which then seemed fantastic.

Wooderson had been a corporal in the Pay Corps for several years, and no one knew how or where he had been able to train. Could he win? Perhaps not, but he had always been a gallant fighter. He ran a great race and battled stride for stride with the great Swede until the last bend. Andersson won in 4 min. 9.4 sec.

As boys we all have our sports heroes, and Wooderson from that day became mine. I admired him as much for his attitude to running as for the feats he achieved. Sydney Wooderson was a methodical and unassuming athlete who was prepared to give up his time and energy to encouraging young athletes even if they showed no promise of outstanding ability. He believed that running was a worthwhile sport in itself, even if one could not achieve any great success. Within the space of a year he had broken the world mile record with a 4 min. 6.4 sec. mile, and set up a new world half-mile record of 1 min. 49.2 sec.

Seeing Wooderson's run that day inspired me with a new interest that has continued ever since. Running is one of the few sports that anyone can do if they are sufficiently determined. Nobody could have wanted to run more than I did.

There is no harm in having ideals. If we aim at a star we may occasionally reach a height normally beyond us. I think we are sometimes wrong to criticise ambition, if we can shelve it when the right moment comes and not become embittered because of failure to reach the target—as I did at school.

So in Oxford I decided to devote a proportion of my time to sport, and if possible to making myself a good runner. In October 1946 I arrived in Oxford, as a Fresh-man at Exeter College. At this time Exeter was a vigor-ous cheerful college with an all-round reputation. The influx of ex-servicemen seemed to have given it a new unity and enthusiasm. E. A. Barber the Rector, Greg Barr the Sub-Rector, and Dacre Balsdon the senior tutor, guided the much travelled ex-servicemen into Oxford's pre-war traditions, and revived the close links between Senior and Junior Common Rooms, between the tutors and the taught.

Without waiting to admire my new college I dropped my bags and set off for the running track. For the first time in the five years I spent in Oxford I made the jour-ney across Magdalen Bridge to the Iffley Road track. I expected to see dozens of brilliant athletes on whom I could feast my eyes in hero worship. I might even be lucky enough to see an Oxford Blue—to me that seemed the height of all achievement. But the track was deserted except for a groundsman who stooped low,

48

coaxing out the daisies as though they were his pet treasures.

This was the track on which three Olympic middle distance runners had trained—Strode-Jackson, Hampson, Lovelock. It was separated from the damp meadows bordering the Isis by a tall row of poplars. It lay peaceful yet defiant, as though unwilling to yield its secret to any who were not prepared to toil up its steep gradient and break their spikes on the rough brick that protruded in places. What should I do? I dared not set foot on the track, I had never run on a track in my life, nor did I dare ask the groundsman where everyone was.

I returned to my college and asked for the Secretary of the Athletic Club. I could only find superior elegant young men, senior undergraduates, I supposed.

"Athletics Secretary? Well really! Have we got one?" Later I realised that they belonged to that select group in Oxford, one of whom had boasted, "Yes, I have occasionally felt the urge to take exercise, but I just lie down until it passes off."

I rummaged about in the dense undergrowth of notices on the college board until I found one that instructed prospective members of the University Athletic Club to send a guinea to the Honorary Secretary at Brasenose College. I went straight to the Post Office and sent off a postal order. Then I returned to college and waited for other freshmen to arrive. I was so impatient to start running that I stood there trying to distinguish the athletes. I hoped to find company in this apparently obscure sport. After a couple of days I began to realise that my tactics were quite wrong. It was not the Oxford method to rush at things. You contemplate, you consider, and then on rare occasions you act.

I found a heavily built oarsman and persuaded him to come for a run. After we had been trotting up and down for half an hour a groundsman came up to talk to the oarsman.

"It's very difficult for me, sir," he said confidentially. "You see, I remember Lovelock well." "Who was he?" I asked. They were both aghast at my ignorance, but I had never heard the name of any world record holders except Wooderson and Gunder Haegg.

"He had such a powerful stride. I think you might become a runner," he said, looking at the oarsman. "But," turning to me, "I'm afraid that you'll never be any good. You just haven't got the strength or the build for it." It seemed as if my hopes were to be killed at the outset.

A week later I received my membership card. Looking back I am still staggered that it ever arrived. Now I felt I could really dare to appear on the track. My running kit must have looked ludicrous to the serious athletes. I still wore the oil-stained outfit I had used for rowing at school, and not having had the importance of warming up explained to me, I did not wear a track suit. It was best to begin quietly.

The Freshmen's Sport were to take place two weeks later. I came across an article on training by Wooderson in which he said, "There is no room for crazy ideas or cranky notions. It consists of just running and plenty of it." This was a simple enough formula to carry in my head, so I trained along the lines of my cross-country preparation in Bath and waited for the great day. I was extremely nervous beforehand and it was one of the few mile races in which I tried to lead from start to finish. I was beaten by an ex-serviceman, Peter Curry, who later represented Britain in the Olympic steeplechase. His time was 4 min. 52 sec., mine 4 min. 53 sec.

It was my first race over a mile. I remember vividly K. S. Duncan, now Secretary of the British Olympic Association, coming up to me afterwards and saying, "Stop bouncing, and you'll knock twenty seconds off." It was the first time I had ever worn running spikes, and they had the effect of making me over-stride in a series of kangaroo-like bounds.

Sandy Duncan was at that time visiting the Iffley Road track once or twice a week, to give the advice and encouragement needed to rebuild Oxford athletics after the lean war years. The time he devoted to those London-Oxford journeys has reaped its benefit in the group of first-class athletes produced at Iffley Road, and in the long sequence of victories in the inter-Varsity match (Oxford has had a run of eight victories beginning in 1948). Other old Blues, Arthur Selwyn, Vernon Scopes and Jerry Cornes, were always at hand to give their advice and assistance. When Peter Curry beat me again in the three miles race a few days later I decided to transfer my energies to cross-country running, which was the main athletic sport during the winter. Peter Curry later gave me every encouragement. He was a good friend whose sense of humour displayed at unpredictable moments helped me to take myself much less seriously.

I ran quite quite well in the inter-college cross-country race and was invited by Eric Mackay, the Captain of Cross-Country, to run with the third University Team. I was overjoyed to receive his selection note. He was a formidable figure—an ex-army captain with a grand manner and a disconcerting way of prefacing all his remarks by the phrase "my dear chap." He usually wore a carnation, and also had the habit, unexpected in an athlete, of being a chain-smoker. It was said he had never been able to last out a three mile race without a friend standing at the 2½ mile mark to give him a puff of his cigarette. The first time I entered his room to deliver my note of acceptance there must have been at least a dozen pairs of suede shoes sticking out from under the bed. Such signs of opulence staggered me.

He kept inviting me to run for the third team over most gruelling 7½ mile courses. I went round to see him, taking back his little note. Each time I said quite firmly, "7½ miles is much too far for me—I want to be a miler and I shall burn myself out."

"Burn yourself out, my dear chap? Of course you won't—it's just the sort of preparation you need. At your age" (he made me feel about ten), "I did lots of 7½

52

mile runs." I refrained from asking whether he thought he had burnt himself out, because he was very kind to me. Time after time I meekly consented to run again the following week. Each time I grew more and more exhausted. I was eventually promoted to the second team, and even won a race, but no one seemed to have noticed. By this time the places in the first team were all filled and my friends were in the second team. Together we shared uncomfortable train journeys, nervous lunches, and the satisfying companionship of mud, rain and barbed wire in the race itself.

But running took only a small part of my time. In my first term in Oxford I only trained once in the middle of the week and raced on Saturdays. The rest of the time I followed my own inclinations, not doing much work. To have reached Oxford was like turning a corner and finding myself unexpectedly in a new world of excitement. I could now satisfy innumerable interests which had been latent throughout the years when I was studying hard at school.

I began to get a first glimpse of the meaning of education and of university life. It was a privilege to sit at the feet of the great men who were lecturing and talking in Oxford. I did not feel out of place as I had at school, where they were always trying to make a man out of me. At Oxford no one seemed to care what became of me and I was heartily content to start at the bottom.

In 1946 ninety per cent of the undergraduates were

ex-servicemen, and then there were a few boys like my-self—it was useless to pretend we were anything else. If they spoke to us and gave us the benefit of their war-time experiences we were surprised and grateful to be noticed. If they chose to ignore us we were not hurt. I sometimes found myself looking innocently puzzled, which indeed I often was, and this made the good advice come more freely. I had so much more to learn than others going up to a university.

At home in the Christmas Vacation life grew more quiet again and I turned to running. I wanted company, and so I joined an athletics club near my own home. I told them, though with what justification I cannot imag-ine, that I hoped to be elected to the Achilles Club the following term. I said I was afraid I would never be able to race for them in matches, as I intended to run pri-marily for the Achilles Club, open only to Oxford and Cambridge athletes.

Unknown to me at the time, by joining the local club first I automatically became "first claim" for them, and I had to resign later in order to become a first claim member of the Achilles Club. This complication, which commonly occurs to other university athletes, often causes unfortunate misunderstanding.

In my case, I was told, the story went round that I was a young runner nurtured and guided by my local club. As I improved I had spurned my early upbringing by the club, and was snatched away by the rapacious Achilles Club. There was not the slightest truth in any of this.

54

Most university athletes would agree that while in residence their primary duty is to their university, though they always like to maintain happy relations with their local clubs.

The only chance I had to race for my local club fell the day after a Hunt Ball to which I had been invited by a fellow cross-country runner. I happily donned my father's dinner jacket. With the trousers at half mast, owing to a discrepancy in our respective heights, I set out for a gay evening, my palate ready for chicken and champagne. I had plenty of both, and went to bed at 5 a.m. When I arrived at the starting line the same day with a hang-over feeling and half-closed eyes, I discovered that D. R. Burfitt, the British junior mile champion, was also running. It was the 1946 Middlesex junior cross-country championships at Enfield Lock, a 5-mile course, and Burfitt had already won the event three times. I had once seen his photograph on the cover of a weekly athletics magazine, so he was already a "star" to me. I managed to stay in second place until the half-way mark, and then my sleepless ill-trained body gave way under the combined strain of the previous night and present exhaustion. I had a violent pain in my side but managed to continue running. I eventually dragged myself over the finishing line in extreme agony in ninth place, but the first member of my club's team to finish. Our team came in second. My award, so hardly won, was a simple medal, the first I received in the greater world, after leaving Bath.

The spring term of 1947 was my first chance to represent Oxford on the track. In those days athletes were just beginning to have training schedules, and I ploughed through the snow one January morning to see Russell Grice, the Secretary of the Athletic Club, who was applying himself devotedly to the creation of a post-war athletics tradition in Oxford. He had very kindly offered to help draw up my schedule. Luckily, the snow and ice were so persistent that I never had a chance to follow it. Otherwise the training schedule would undoubtedly have killed me, it was so stenuous. Instead I learned to skate on Port Meadow for a week or two before returning to Iffley Road and helping to shovel away the snow so that the track could be used.

At about this time I discovered that to a few undergraduates in Oxford, athletics was a full-time occupation. Gradually I recognised them in and about Oxford from having seen them at the track. They were Blues, Half-Blues, and "Centipedes," a club comprising fifty members, or, if you prefer it, a hundred "feet." Their day seemed to go something like this—morning coffee at the "Kemp," lunch in the "Stowaway," the whole afternoon at the track, tea at the "Angel" and dinner at "Vincents." They usually rounded off their strenuous day with an evening's relaxation at the cinema. I was amazed and shocked. I had been brought up to regard it as a crime to waste time. These athletes never seemed to visit lecture room or laboratory, and seldom to enter their colleges. It worried me to think that I might be expected to join

56

them if ever I ran well enough to become a Blue. There did not seem to be any great danger of this at the time.

One day I overheard a conversation at the track about Jack Lovelock coming down to give a talk to the "possibles" for the match against Cambridge at the end of the term. The Secretary had once invited me inside the Blues' changing room at the Pavilion, and I had seen, hanging over the mantelpiece, a photograph of Lovelock winning the 1936 Olympic 1,500 metres race in Berlin. I felt hurt that I was not invited, and wondered whether I dared wait at the track in the hope of seeing the great runner even if I could not hear him speak. I decided to keep my pride and to stay away from the track on that day.

The snow persisted, so no trials to choose the team were possible. Anyone available who competed the previous year was selected automatically. This left the third string in the mile to be chosen. The President had seen me training and selected me from a bunch of "also rans" on this slight recommendation.

A Blue has no longer quite the distinction it used to have. Now that undergraduates cannot afford to go down from Oxford with no degree, or even an inferior one, sport takes second place to work. The picture of a noisy crowd of Blues parading crested sweaters, almost invisible beneath yards of coloured scarfing, as they wander from Vincents to Iffley Road, is now out of date.

57

Old Blues say, "Oxford is not what it was." It never is.

I now had my half Blue, provided I managed to avoid catching measles or falling downstairs before the following Saturday. The University Sports are always planned like a great military battle. I was only third string, and my orders were to move into the lead if the Cambridge runners failed to set the right pace. Otherwise I could run my own race.

Saturday, 22nd March 1947 at the White City, was a cold wet day, the sort of day on which the Sports invariably fall—according to the vast experience of Old Blues. It was the second meeting after a wartime interval of six years. The track was of the consistency of lumpy porridge, it was so soaked by the rain. I felt that the honour of my University was at stake and the responsibility weighed heavily on my shoulders, despite the fact that only a handful of spectators had come to the meeting. This was, after all, the White City Stadium, where I had seen Wooderson running two years before.

When the gun fired, the Cambridge runners shot into the lead so I stayed back at a respectful distance and remained there until the middle of the back straight after the bell. I was as tired as everyone else, but suddenly for the first time I felt a crazy desire to overtake the whole field. I raced through into the lead and a feeling of great mental and physical excitement swept over me. I forgot my tiredness. I suddenly tapped that hidden source of energy I always suspected I possessed. I won by twenty yards in a time of 4 min. 30.8 sec.

I had expressed something of my attitude to life in the only way it could be expressed, and it was this that gave me the thrill. It was intensity of living, joy in struggle, freedom in toil, satisfaction at the mental and physical cost. It gave me a glimpse of the future because I had discovered my gift for running—an unconscious conspiracy of mind and body that made this energy release possible. I knew from that day that I could develop this newly found ability.

My confidence was quite restored. I could almost have stopped running at that moment, like so many athletes with unfulfilled promise, who decide to give their time to other things. They can do this because they have discovered a new source of power and at the same time achieved some degree of mastery over themselves. But I was not content with this. I had at that moment the freedom to stop or go on. If I went on, then I must not allow passing disappointments at a later stage to prevent me from achieving all that I felt I could achieve.

It is still a mystery quite what happened to me the evening after my first White City race. I prefer that it should always remain in a state of blissful haze, so that no detail can mar the perfect happiness I felt on being an assured Blue. The only incident of athletic importance that evening was my first meeting with Jack Lovelock. I blinked unsteadily.

"You mean *the* Jack Lovelock?" I said, and shook his hand so vigorously that I upset his glass. Perhaps it is significant that I remember my first meeting with Lovelock though I cannot remember when I first met Wooderson. Yet Wooderson, my boyish ideal, could never be displaced, and I accepted him uncritically as a runner of genius.

Lovelock I could meet on more equal terms. He intrigued me. At this time his health was not good, and a riding accident had affected his sight. Someone who was with him at the time said that he suddenly rode off alone from the rest of the field while hunting, and was not picked up until some hours later.

It was sheer coincidence that I was at the same college in Oxford, and later at the same hospital in London. I had not heard of him until I went up to Oxford. There he was looked upon as a master of relaxation, the cleverest, neatest miler they had ever seen. His consummate victory in Berlin in 1936 was enough to fill any athlete with admiration. For the next few years I never missed the opportunity of talking to those who had known him. Shortly after this first meeting he went to live in America, where we met again two years later.

Another great British athlete and former Olympic champion I met for the first time that evening was Harold Abrahams, who has made such a great contribution to the popularity of athletics in this country, both by his writing and broadcasting. On this occasion he noted my promise, and it was the beginning of a close friendship which has continued throughout my athletic career. His advice has been invaluable to me on all occasions when important decisions have had to be made.

# CHAPTER FIVE

# OXFORD — GRADUATION

*"If you want to get somewhere else, you must
run at least twice as fast as that."*
THROUGH THE LOOKING GLASS.

HAVING WON MY FULL BLUE, I drifted more into the
company of sportsmen, though I still retained the wider
interests of my first two terms. I had always been puzzled by the mysterious institution called "Vincents"—to
which the more pleasant and sociable athletes would dis-
appear when overwhelmed by great success or failure. I
now discovered it was a club, with premises over a print-
er's shop from which it took its name. The members
were mainly sportsmen—sport tends to produce a more
sociable person than pure scholarship. There were few
full Blues who were not members, so my fellow athletes
were keen to have me elected. I was absurdly young for
such an honour and felt supremely "unclubbable."

One day I was taken there to dine by a Committee
member, R. T. S. MacPherson. He had been awarded a
Military Cross with two bars for his service in Italy.
Later he gained an athletics Blue and played in the University and London Scottish Rugby XVs. My visit to

Vincents was presumably for inspection by the Club's Committee to determine whether one so young could be a fit and proper person for admission to membership. I quaked at finding myself in company with such Oxford heroes—in my nervousness I upset my tankard and hardly ate anything. I heard later that I had been elected a member.

For nearly a year I hardly dared to go inside the Club. Sometimes I would mount the stairs and quickly look round the lounge. If there was no one I knew I would glance at the headlines of a newspaper or hurriedly write a note, and then rush out again. I had such veneration for the Club's tradition that I was quite unable to relax in it. Three years later when I was President of the Club and lived in a room there, I found Vincents one of Oxford's most enjoyable institutions. It was another kind of graduation, in advance of my academic one.

After getting my Blue I was made Secretary of the Centipede Club and given some responsibility for organising matches. I embarked on an ambitious programme of two meetings a week—many being "away" matches. I competed in few of them because I had a morbid fear of burning myself out. I knew that I could probably drive myself hard enough to do well in these meetings. But I knew also that it was unwise to attempt this if I wanted to have a future as a runner—if I wanted to do well in the Olympic Games. So instead I concentrated mainly on organising the matches for other athletes.

At Oxford against the A.A.A.* on 5th June 1947, I ran a 4 min. 24.6 sec. mile at the age of eighteen—faster than Wooderson at the same age. But standards change quickly. In 1954 Roger Dunkley ran a mile in 4 min. 12.8 sec., also at eighteen. The improvement seems fantastic, but I am not so sure that training of the intensity required to produce such a remarkable time is a good thing at that age.

In August of 1947 I had my first trip abroad. It was the first occasion since the war that British and German athletes had met. The standard of living in Germany was very low at the time. The Germans ran badly, or dropped out of races longer than a mile, and we wondered whether this was really genuine or was intended to impress us with their lack of stamina due to inadequate food. In contrast, a one-legged German cleared the high jump at 5 ft. 10 in., and beat our own athletes.

At Cologne the temperature was 100° in the shade, and there was not a breath of wind. We stood to attention for the interminable speech of the bearded bespectacled Mayor, and had a taste of the German cheering methods which had been so unpopular in the Berlin Olympic Stadium in 1936.

John Wilkinson, who had come up to Oxford that summer, accompanied us. He was 100 Yards Public School champion and a famous schoolboy international rugby player. He was the "discovery" of the tour. Though eighteen like myself he was much more mature

* Amateur Athletic Association.

64

and definitely of greater potentiality. John was a supreme example of the light-hearted approach to athletics. Whatever the meeting he was never rattled at the starting point. He bore with unfailing good humour the disappointment of having to follow McDonald Bailey to the tape in so many races that summer. It was a great misfortune that a rugby injury in 1948 kept him out of the Wembley Olympics. He ran the fastest ever 200 metres for a United Kingdom athlete, when he set up a time of 21.3 sec. in Cologne, and then went on to Paris to win the 100 and 200 metres titles in the World Student Games.

At this stage my interest in running waned. I was resting heavily on my youthful laurels and expected promise. There was no challenge at Oxford or Cambridge, and I had no wish to enter national or international competition. Had I done so I am sure it would have affected my ability at a later date. Like most first year undergraduates I only worked when I could find nothing more exciting to do—which I usually could. I showed the usual tendency at this age to become a dilettante.

I tried hard to find a coach. Athletic coaches developed from the old handyman-masseur trainer at the end of last century—they were the bath attendant coaches who gradually pick up "tips" by their acute observation. They had great practical knowledge and judgment. Some were successful runners in their day.

Bill Thomas belonged to this school and was coach for

65

many years to the Oxford University Athletic Club. Lovelock had great confidence in him. I went along to see him, and he stood by the track, bowler-hatted, watching me run round. He grunted continuously but said little. Though the comments he made were probably extremely shrewd, he seemed upset when I asked him why he said this or that. I think he worked intuitively and I needed reasons for the things I did. As I left him I felt disappointed. Lovelock no doubt had faith based on a need of his help, but somehow I did not feel my need so strongly.

Bill Thomas's successor at Oxford was John Jeffery, who typified the new post-war group of coaches, who have done so much to raise the standard of British athletic achievement, particularly in field events, where we have for so long lagged behind European and American athletes. Under the leadership of Geoffrey Dyson, the A.A.A. and club coaches have cast their net over the whole country, ensuring as far as possible that no potential talent is wasted for lack of adequate guidance and instruction. Much is yet to be done, but the effect of this systematic coaching policy is seen each year in the rising standard of British athletics and in the number of well trained young athletes.

Athletes are sometimes hard to restrain. In November 1947, after winning the relays at Cambridge, our team became merry, if not unruly. Our President was not there to keep control. He was late for the coach which was to take us back to Oxford, and the Secretary was in

Oxford to take exams. This left me as the only one who had any official status, but I was too young to restrain anyone.

The team grew more and more impatient until a shout of "souvenirs" went up. Half the team left the coach and began to tear down any traffic signs that looked removable, and to make attempts on some that resisted all their efforts. A crowd gathered to watch their attempts to remove a "Halt" sign that was electrically lit. This fused all the lights along the street, and someone called the Police.

Just as we managed to get the enthusiasts back in the coach and were driving off, leaving the President behind, the headlights of a Police Squad on motor cycles swung into the road from both directions, and our escape was blocked. Before we were allowed to leave we had to assume joint responsibility for the damage by handing them a list of our names.

In the weeks before we received the bill, Cambridge friends would write to tell how many men were working on the restoration of the "Halt" sign. When the bill did come we suspected that half the signs in Cambridge must have been replaced.

Owing to a resignation I became Secretary of the Oxford Athletic Club in January 1948, and for a time my running took second place to the organisation of the Club. The administrative work of running a Club of 200 members for the benefit of 25 colleges is almost too much for an undergraduate to perform unassisted with-

67

out his work suffering. It was lucky that I was not expected to hold office for longer than three months. In this brief period I realised the amount of work which had to be done, and it made me appreciate the loyalty and efficiency of Derek Steel who succeeded me as Secretary during my term of office as President. I knew little of Derek when he was elected, except that he was older than I, and had spent some time at the Sorbonne in Paris. I soon found that he had an inexhaustible fund of good sense, and he prevented me from making mistakes in administration and team planning.

During my apprenticeship I came to identify myself completely with the University approach to sport and athletics. I was fascinated when I began to look into the reasons for the success of the system. No one could deny that it was successful—the Achilles Club had produced twelve Olympic champions since 1920, and *Time* magazine has characteristically distilled the essence of the spirit behind this achievement in a headline, "Athletes for fun." As this was the only approach I had known I found it difficult to take an unbiased attitude.

Even before the war the balance of athletic prestige in this country had shifted away from the older universities, which at one time provided the majority of the country's athletes. University athletes formerly confined themselves to university events, which provide strenuous competition throughout the year, summer and winter. They suffer from unremitting efforts to maintain racing fitness in the middle of winter, when the university relays and cross-country fixtures are held. Now most of them attempt to reach a further peak for national and international competition in the late summer.

Most university athletes belong also to local athletic clubs, and I am convinced that their approach can be helpful to all clubs. The university method has had great success yet is apparently casual. This contradiction puzzles many people.

Undergraduates are, without exception, haunted by the fear of being thought to take anything too seriously. I know that I developed the pose of apparent indifference, to hide the tremendous enthusiasm which I felt for running, from the day I set foot in Oxford. You had to be almost as careful in Oxford not to appear to take games too seriously as you had at school to avoid the stigma of being called a "swot."

Behind this general façade I found I could quickly learn a great deal about training. This was regarded as a highly individual affair. Nothing is sacred in Oxford and every training programme was attacked and analysed. There was no slavish adherence to outmoded dogma or athletic ritual as there seemed to be in the rowing world. I developed a form of training, running perhaps for half an hour, three or four times a week, which seemed to give reasonable results, without making life a misery.

Running thrives in an atmosphere of interplay of ideas about training. I have always learned more from other athletes than from professional coaches who have never been runners themselves. Though highly qualified in the

69

technique of the events, coaches sometimes have diffi-culty in applying their textbook information.

There is no established technique for running. It was thousands of years from the time when cave men at-tempted to draw running movements, before the cinema camera accurately analysed the relation of arms and legs in motion. But this in itself has produced no great im-provement in running. The human body is centuries in advance of the physiologist, and can perform an integra-tion of heart, lungs and muscles which is too complex for the scientist to analyse.

Improvement in running depends on continuous self-discipline by the athlete himself, on acute observation of his reaction to races and training, and above all on judg-ment, which he must learn for himself. The runner has to make his own decisions on the track—he has no coach there to help him. If a man coaches himself then he has only himself to blame when he is beaten.

My ideal athlete was first and foremost a human being who ran his sport and did not allow it to run him. He was not a racehorse nor a professional strong man. He drank beer, he might smoke, and he listened to coaches when he felt inclined. With so many other interests and activities there was no danger of mental staleness. The man who mumbled about his weight chart and his pulse ratio was left to the tender mercies of his fellow fanatics. All this may be wrong; but it had already produced twelve Olympic champions—men whose personality and determination were sufficient to enable them to plan successful athletic careers and at the same time to achieve balanced lives.

Throughout the year college athletics provided light relief from the more serious university matches. An ill assorted medley of college games-players turned their hands to athletic events with varying success. My own college, Exeter, had great enthusiasm in the immediate post-war years. A flourishing college bar provided fruitful ground for the athletic press gang looking for recruits. When R. C. Barkway, later Olympic hurdler, was college captain we won the inter-college relay cup and were second in the inter-college sports. Both successes were hilariously celebrated.

In April 1948, though I was still almost the youngest member of the team, I was elected President of the University Athletic Club. I was still trying to conquer my shyness and slowly improving. But as soon as I became President my old worries returned. Though I had ideas of what should be done, I doubted whether I could do the job effectively.

It all came to a climax at my first speech in Worcester College Hall just after my election. The whole club was assembled and the Senior Treasurer, Alan Brown, a fellow of Worcester and later Mayor of Oxford, was sitting next to me. As the election was unopposed I had carefully written out my speech in full beforehand. I had self-consciously rehearsed it aloud in my room that morning. Now I lost my nerve. After struggling through the first few sentences my head began to swim. I blurted

71

out disjointed phrases that I had memorised, but entirely lost the thread of the points I was attempting to make. I continually repeated myself. As I stood there, blushing uncomfortably and getting more and more confused, the only clear thought that passed through my mind was, "What a fool you are making of yourself—letting down the trust shown in you. How they must wish they had never elected you President."

I managed to come to my senses in time. In front of everyone I tore up the paper on which I had written my speech. I made a feeble joke about being used to running, not to making speeches, and started saying what I really felt. You don't need to be an orator to do that. Any appearance of confident oratory I had hoped to make had failed miserably. The barriers were down between myself and the club, so I had nothing to lose by starting again. If my election as President had not improved me, it had at any rate not made me any worse. To my amazement, when I tried again the words came freely and sincerely.

My plans for the club were very ambitious. I had schemes for raising the membership and providing coaching by a professional. This was a revolutionary step, but Oxford had come to rely too much on sportsmen from Europe and the Dominions, especially in field events. This however hardly justified the remarks made after the 1949 Varsity rugby match—"the British Empire against Cambridge!" The system of coaching by reign-

72

ing Blues seemed only to produce results in the running events and hurdles, and so was inadequate.

I hoped that the American tours by Oxford and Cambridge teams would be revived.

I had got going now. I said I would not rest until plans were started to replace the old ⅓-mile track with a new six-lane 440 yards track conforming to international specifications.

At this point the Senior Treasurer gave me a pained look. I said that the existing track was a disgrace to a university that had produced so many fine athletes. They had succeeded in spite of, rather than with the help of the facilities provided. This was nothing to be proud of.

The present track was like a cross-country course, though not as bad as the Cambridge track at Fenners! We did not know quite what happened round the bottom bend behind the long grass. The runners disappeared down the nine foot drop on the back straight before they climbed the hill to the finish. We only thought it strange that a different runner often emerged first! I was tired of being told that Lovelock had run a 4 min. 12 sec. mile on this old track.

As the year went by I won some support for the idea of a new track. To pacify old Blues who thought the scheme too revolutionary I said, "Don't worry, we will still run round the opposite way to anyone else!" It was then that I first heard the ingenious Strode-Jackson theory of how Oxford produces her middle distance runners. By running clockwise they strengthened the left leg more

73

than the right. Assuming that the right leg is naturally stronger this method should result in an even level stride —the secret of success!

The Senior Treasurer patiently bore the responsibility for my enthusiasm, and without his guidance and support the plan would never have been started. We had great difficulty in overcoming the opposition of the University football club, whose pitch occupied the centre of the track. They said they could not possibly manage with anything less than a full size pitch, which could not be contained under the new scheme within a 440-yard track. At the crucial meeting, when the plan was to be accepted or rejected, we asked them if they would regard the football pitches used by the Arsenal and some other First Division clubs as adequate. None of these was in fact full size, and we won the day.

The work began. As I stood amid the bulldozers, the piles of clay and the dying turf that summer, I resolved that if ever the track was finished I would choose it for my biggest races. Two years later the new track was opened by the Vice-Chancellor.

# CHAPTER SIX

# OLYMPIC GAMES

## WEMBLEY 1948

*"Faith, I ran when I saw others run."*
HENRY V, PART I.

IN NOVEMBER 1947 I received an invitation to become a "possible" for the Olympic Games to be held at Wembley in the following summer. The "possibles" were to receive assistance which ranged from special coaching organised by the Amateur Athletic Association, to food parcels given by the Dominions to supplement their limited rations.

I felt I was not ready at the time for competition of Olympic standard. Though I might possibly survive these tense conditions and even reach the final, I thought it would prejudice my chances for the 1952 Games. So I declined the invitation to become a "possible"—though the A.A.A. still allowed me to receive some of the benefits. It never occurred to me that there was anything strange in my action—it seemed the only sensible course. My decision received considerable publicity—"Bannister says he's too young."

I won my second Oxford-Cambridge mile at the White City on 20th March 1948 in 4 min. 23.4 sec., taking the lead after 600 yards. My first race as President of the Oxford Club was in the Universities Athletic Union championships at Motspur Park on 22nd May 1948. I did not take the lead decisively enough before the last bend and was nearly overtaken by a surprise rush from J. W. McKay, the Irish rugby forward. My time was 4 min. 23.8 sec., and I was only saved by thrusting out my chest at the tape.

On 19th June 1948 I ran in my first crowded mile field for the Achilles Club in the Kinnaird Mile at the Chiswick Stadium. I started somewhere in the second row, and most of the race was a battle of elbows. Douglas Wilson, R. A. Morris and Alec Olney burst through at the finish. I came fourth, but my time of 4 min. 18.7 sec. came quite easily, although it was my fastest to date. I had allowed myself to drop so far back at the beginning of the last lap that it would have been difficult to make good the loss.

My running was going so well that I began to doubt my wisdom in withdrawing from Olympic selection. Perhaps I had been foolish in thinking that I was too young. I was gambling on a future improvement as an athlete that might never come. So I wavered in my decision.

I entered for the A.A.A. Mile Championship in 1948, my first appearance in competition at this level. I thought that if I ran well I might still be considered for

76

Olympic selection. But I hesitated about forcing myself to run flat out. The race was won by Nankeville in 4 min. 14.2 sec., with Barthel of Luxembourg second, De Ruyter of Belgium third, Morris fourth and myself fifth. My time was my fastest to that date, 4 min. 17.2 sec. I was the third Englishman, a significant position, as there were three places to be filled for the Olympic 1,500 metres. Douglas Wilson did not run owing to a muscle injury, and he was selected as Britain's third representative. Douglas Wilson was the only athlete besides Sydney Wooderson whom I had watched as a schoolboy. I had seen him running an exhibition ¾-mile trial at Headstone Lane track near my home in Harrow, and at that time almost looked upon him as superhuman. Looking back I feel very relieved on the whole that I did not earn selection for the 1948 Olympics.

The Olympic Games at Wembley were the great event of the summer. I was appointed assistant to the Commandant of the British team, Col. E. A. Hunter, O.B.E. My duties ranged from delivering letters to conducting distinguished visitors round the Olympic village at Uxbridge.

One anxious moment stands out. On 29th July 1948 the day of the opening ceremony, the Commandant and I were about to drive over to the Stadium. We had been told that a car carrying the flags of all the nations was to drive along the line of assembled teams just before they marched into the Stadium. In this way there would be no danger of any team forgetting its flag. As we were

77

leaving Uxbridge my eyes caught sight of an old Union Jack which we had used for minor flag-raising ceremonies. We kept it rolled up in a corner of the office. I suggested we should take it with us, "just in case."

On arrival at Wembley we saw the car park was crowded and we left it to the driver to find a place. The Commandant and I made our way to the British team. The flags for the parade had just been handed out—there was no flag for the British team. A mistake had been made. In another twenty minutes the British team, parading last as host nation, would enter the Stadium. The whole ceremony culminated in placing the flags of the various countries in a semi-circle round an athlete who would take the Olympic oath on behalf of all competitors.

The Commandant ordered me to find the flag we had brought from Uxbridge. He gave me a jeep and a British Army sergeant. Together we tore off towards the car park. We drove furiously through the crowds which still packed the approaches to the Stadium. I kept my hand on the hooter so that it sounded continuously. We reached the car park. There were thousands of cars and we had not the faintest idea where ours was.

Everyone stared as we rushed like madmen up and down the lines of cars. It took us ten minutes to find our car. It was locked, so I smashed a window with a stone while the sergeant restrained a policeman who wanted to arrest me.

Seizing the flag I rushed back to the jeep, and we set

78

off for the Stadium. But the entrances were blocked by last minute arrivals and the jeep was soon hemmed in on all sides. Hooting was useless. Time was desperately short, and I could see the British team having to parade without a flag. I jumped out of the jeep. Using the flag as a battering ram, with brass spike foremost, I charged through the crowd and reached the British team just before they marched into the Stadium.

It was a hot sunny day, and 80,000 people had assembled in the gaily bedecked Stadium. I had the feeling that we were witnessing sacred rites being performed in an open air cathedral. The crowd hushed as an anonymous youth, clad in white, completed a circuit of the track, holding a torch with the Olympic flame that had been carried all the way from Greece.

It was J. W. E. Mark, the tall blond Cambridge 440 and 880 yards runner, who had been President of the Cambridge University Athletic Club in 1947, when I first competed for Oxford.

The flame would burn night and day in the Stadium while the Games lasted. It had been carried by relays of runners from the sacred olive grove at Olympus where it had been kindled two weeks before from the sun's rays at noon. A Greek girl with her escort of young men had carried the flame across the river Altis to the spot where the heart of Baron de Coubertin, the founder of the modern Olympic Games, lies buried.

The first runner was a corporal in the Greek Army. He had laid down his arms and taken off his uniform to

appear clad as an athlete, thus symbolising the tradition
that war ceased during the period of the Games. Then
he had lit his torch from the first flame and set off on his
stage of the relay. Now the flame was springing to life
in Wembley Stadium, its journey completed. It was the
flame of idealism, a symbol of hope and striving, an inspiration to all young people.

Lord Burghley, Chairman of the Organising Committee, invited King George VI to declare the Games
open:—

"The hour has struck. A visionary dream has today
become a glorious reality. . . . These Games are a living
proof of this great common bond of sportsmanship that
binds the youth of the world together. . . . When a great
cause marches hand in hand with sincerity and enthusiasm, none can stop its progress."

In his dedicatory address the Archbishop of York
said:—

"No victory in the Games can be gained without the
moral qualities of self-control and self-discipline. . . .
Honour is due not only to the victors but also to the defeated, if in the true spirit of sportsmanship they give at
once ungrudging and generous praise to those who have
surpassed them in skill and endurance. For, by so doing,
though beaten in the contest, they show mastery over
themselves . . . when the Games are over, those who
have taken part in them should return to their homes as
torch bearers . . . with the flame of goodwill burning in
their hearts, and continuing to burn there long after the
Olympic Flame has been extinguished."

Then Wing-Commander Donald Finlay, Captain of the British team, took the oath on behalf of the athletes, that they would "take part in the Olympic Games in loyal competition . . . desirous of participating in them in the true spirit of sportsmanship, for the honour of our country and for the glory of sport."

The Olympic Games of 1948 changed my whole outlook. Until this time I had been inclined to look on athletics as a personal affair. I saw in it primarily a way of achieving that mastery over myself which I felt I was always in danger of losing—as I had done at school. I hoped my striving as an athlete would liberate other potentialities which I knew existed inside me. Some of these I had discovered. During the last year I had grown worried that the rigours of training and the strain of competition might dull my sensitivity to other things in life.

But when I was caught up in the Olympic movement this fear vanished. I grew outside my own feeble preoccupations and strivings on the track and was transported to a greater realisation of the true significance of sport. Sport changed from being a jumbled striving of individual athletes and teams to a new unity, with a beauty that is evident in man's highest endeavour. In all this I felt proud to have a small part.

Many of the principles that I had learnt in Oxford and thought to be Oxford's special contribution to sport I now discovered had existed for over two thousand years. The debt of loyalty that I had reserved for Oxford I now

81

found I owed to a whole world of sport that was born
with the Olympic movement and was rejuvenated with
each Olympic Games.

The Greek ideal was that sport should be a preparation
for life in general. Physical perfection was a worthy end,
and the striving heightened rather than dulled percep-
tion of other things. The Greeks were stimulated by the
idea of competition. They believed that competition,
whether in music or drama, in art or poetry, brought out
the best in man. It was for the victors at the Olympic
Games that Pindar wrote many of his odes. The Greeks
believed that men should take pleasure in toil and struggle. There was a certain magic in victory that transformed not only the victor but also the defeated.

The aim of the Greek Olympics was the improvement
of the whole man. For a long time specialisation was
discouraged. Athletes, even if not themselves scholars,
competed within a stone's throw of the auditorium
where dramatic performances took place. Before he
turned traitor, Alcibiades was a fine example of the athlete who was also a writer and thinker. Bodily perfection
was an essential part of the highest culture, on a level
with music and poetry.

Like all good ideas, competition could be harmful
when carried to excess. Greek individualism in sport was
akin to the individualism that was the bane of their politics. There came a time when Greek sport decayed.
This took several well defined stages.

Success became so important for the prestige of a city

state that the city was not too scrupulous about the means of achieving it. This was followed by over-emphasis on competition. The idea of the all-rounder, sound mind in sound body, was lost, and specialisation set in. The professional athlete emerged, without any other occupation. This was fatal to the "amateur" spirit.

When he revived the ancient Olympic Games in 1896, Baron de Coubertin was responsible for modifying the emphasis on individuality and victory—"The important thing in the Olympic Games is not winning but taking part. The essential thing in life is not conquering but fighting well."

These were some of my thoughts as I watched the 1948 Olympic Games. I wondered in particular whether the Games were in danger of changing their nature. Was a new form of professionalism creeping in, with the athlete maintained by his country for purposes of prestige? Might not the Olympic Games accentuate the political struggle between the different nations? At the beginning of each Games such questions are raised. Then they are forgotten as the moving drama of success and failure unrolls itself.

I saw Zatopek's genius revealed for the first time with his runaway victory in the 10,000 metres. I wondered what went on in his mind when he allowed Gaston Reiff of Belgium to set up an enormous lead in the 5,000 metres, and then set off to catch him in the last lap—but too late. It almost looked as though he were staging a most dramatic coup, which only failed by a yard.

83

I watched Barney Ewell, the confident Negro American sprinter, dance with joy and even commiserate with the other competitors when he imagined he had won the 100 metres, only to discover that he was second. Harrison Dillard, better known as a hurdler, had won.

I saw Donald Finlay, aged 42, after one of the greatest hurdling careers, trip over the last hurdle in his heat.

I remember Arthur Wint's breakdown with muscle cramp in the 4 × 400 metres relay, when he was struggling to catch the Americans. This was perhaps the most moving and tragic moment in the whole Games. Within the space of a week Wint had completed the first round, semi-final and Final of the 800 metres, being placed second behind the American Mal Whitfield in the Final. He followed this by a sequence of two rounds, semi-final and Final of the 400 metres, snatching victory in the last few strides from the favourite, his fellow Jamaican and world record holder, Herb McKenley.

Now with McKenley in his own team he was attempting to win the 4 × 400 metres relay title for the tiny island of Jamaica against the massed forces of the American team. Much as we all admired the good sportsmanship and unfailing efficiency of the American athletes, we had grown a little weary of hearing the "Stars and Stripes" played at successive victory ceremonies. We hoped that with a Jamaican victory we might hear the British National Anthem, followed perhaps by an unofficial calypso from the West Indian spectators.

It was the old story of the crowd's sympathies being

84

with the small man against the giant, though these terms applied only to the geography and population of Jamaica and the United States. No one in the American team could overtop the two giants, Wint and McKenley.

Rhoden was the first runner for Jamaica and finished level with his American opponent, Harnden. The second Jamaican runner Laing, a sprinter gallantly trying to race twice his normal distance, handed over to Wint twelve yards behind Cochran, the American Olympic 400 metres hurdles champion. Could Wint and Mc-Kenley win this margin back from Cochran and Whit-field? It seemed unlikely, but the crowd, always ready to sympathise with challengers, shouted their encouragement as Wint set off after his man. With enormous strides he flashed round the first bend. Normally Arthur Wint's running seemed deceptively slow, but this time there was no mistaking his speed and urgency.

As he entered the back straight he gained on Cochran with each stride, but suddenly his body convulsed and he flung himself on the grass verge, his face distorted with the agony of a searing muscle pull. I almost clutched my own thigh, the injury seemed so real and personal; an injury that I myself was not to experience until five years later. I did not see Cochran steaming home to give Whitfield a commanding lead, but remained staring at the prostrate figure of Arthur Wint, thumping the turf with baton and fist in exasperation, oblivious to the comforting enquiries of his fellow Jamaicans. In that moment I realised the frustration that

85

comes when the body breaks beneath the compelling demands of the will to victory.

This final Saturday of the Games was a day of tragedy and mistakes. For a moment it seemed as though the British 4 × 100 metres relay team had won a gold medal for first place, awarded when the U.S.A. team was disqualified for an alleged faulty changeover. It would have been a most unsatisfactory triumph, and we were all relieved when the decision was later reversed. No athlete is content to take a prize accruing from a rival's misfortune.

The last event, the Marathon, was a tragedy for the Belgium athlete, E. Gailly. He was the first to return to the Stadium. Staggering on the final circuit of the track, he was passed by the Argentinian, D. Cabrera, and Tom Richards from Wales. The sharp stinging challenge in the final lap of a mile race can be distressing, but I prefer it to the long-drawn-out agony of a Marathon. I should never have the patience to endure the strain of the race, and above all the monotony of the endless road training. I have often wondered how runners like Jim Peters and Jack Holden inure themselves to the demands their sport makes upon them.

Of the three British entrants for the 1,500 metres, Nankeville reached the Final. His time of 3 min. 52.6 sec. gave him sixth place, and was one of the fastest recorded until then by a British runner. The strength of the European, and particularly the Swedish, middle distance runners at Wembley came as a surprise to many

86

of us. H. Eriksson of Sweden won the gold medal with a time of 3 min. 49.8 sec., and his countrymen L. Strand and G. Bergkvist took second and fifth places.

It was apparent that the times which would win mile and 3-mile titles at the White City were not fast enough to win races against international class athletes. New targets had to be set and more vigorous training programmes prepared. This was one of the lessons which I learned as a spectator at Wembley.

By the end of the Games I was restless and anxious to compete myself. There were four years to wait before my chance would come at Helsinki in 1952. I decided I could allow myself two years of carefree running before I started single-minded preparation for Helsinki. I expected the standard would be higher then, but I hoped to be better prepared.

# CHAPTER SEVEN

# FIRST TOUR IN AMERICA

## *1949*

*"Go west, young man."*
J. B. L. SOULE (1851).

SOONER OR LATER we undertake an adventure that may change our lives. For me it came when I first went to the United States. America had previously seemed as far off to me as a third year medical student as dinner at the Savoy might to a beggar on the Embankment.

We had been trying to revive the athletics matches which had taken place before the war against the American Universities of Princeton, Cornell, Yale and Harvard—the Ivy League, as it is called. I dared not hope for too much in case the plans went astray. But early in June 1949 we found ourselves climbing on board a Strato-cruiser at London Airport. I was flying for the first time—as Captain of a combined Oxford-Cambridge team.

I felt the thrill of powerful engines revving up and being held back by the brakes. The plane feels hopelessly heavy as it taxies across the runway. Suddenly you see fields and hedges below and you have taken off. The earth slips behind, becomes smaller—details of town and countryside are blurred. You feel as though you yourself have performed the trick of levitation. Flying is mostly boring, but at times it can be exciting. With England left behind there were hours when scintillation from the sky-blue ocean seemed to flash from the silver wing tips. Just when the monotony seemed unbearable the plane was encircled with an ever changing pattern of cloud. We flew out above the cloud, and saw it below with a golden lining reflecting the sun.

Again there was monotony until the clouds cleared. Someone spotted an iceberg. The plane crossed the black, almost cruel, forests of Newfoundland—occasional glacial lakes looking like gigantic footprints, as if some monster had spanned the country in a few strides.

As our plane climbed, it kept pace with the sunset. For a moment we defeated the geometry of space, racing the earth and keeping night at bay. The sun, careworn from the day and unable to sink beyond our vision, seemed to flatten in fitful sulkiness. Then, finally enraged, it threw upwards a flaming band before it dropped silently into tomorrow, leaving the night to us.

I was looking forward to my races in America with a mixture of anxiety and pleasure. I had spent the summer in England, training to reach my peak in America. In my last time trial, a half-mile for the A.A.A. against London University at Motspur Park on 1st June 1949, I ran the distance in 1 min. 52.7 sec., nearly 5 seconds

89

improvement on my previous best time. I felt in good heart.

America has a gift for taking up outsiders and making them feel at home. I have never entirely lost the feeling of freedom that living in America for two months gave me—freedom to look at life in a different way. We do not see Americans in Europe at their best. Sometimes they irritate us by an over-assertiveness brought out perhaps by their sense of strangeness when confronted with traditions they themselves lack.

I was continually startled by the Americans' alertness and interest in life. Apathy is less common than in England; there it is no crime to be enthusiastic. I was continually being jolted out of my complacency by an apt remark from someone I thought half asleep. In sport Americans suddenly spring to life and beat their opponents with an off-hand smile.

At Princeton we hit the re-union, or rather it hit us. The students had only just held their celebration parties and had hardly given up their bottle-strewn rooms. The Oxford-Cambridge team moved into some of them, and the remainder were taken over by the "alumni," old boys of the University returning for their annual re-union.

Whatever had been their degree of success in life these former students had come back for a week to share memories and so grow young again. Each "class," numbered according to its year of graduation, wore a special fancy dress, for which the black and orange colours of the University provided the theme. No British University has

90

such "class" pride. This mellow mood of re-dedication no doubt produced an atmosphere which encouraged generous subscriptions to the University for the benefit of successive generations of students.

At Princeton we could easily have imagined ourselves in parts of Oxford or Cambridge—except that the stone of the buildings was new and clean. Just when we were feeling at home again there would be a whiff of white smoke from mock Gothic turrets, and we realised that the historic looking building was only the laundry. As we visualised a yeoman soldier guarding a Tudor archway, a gay alumnus, dressed in a gaudy orange and black zoot-suit, and wearing a jockey cap, would wander past.

I met Lovelock at Princeton for the second time. Here he ran his epic race in 1933 against Bill Bonthron, when he set up a new world record of 4 min. 7.6 sec. Our conversation was short, but he advised me when to use my finishing burst to the most telling advantage. He said that in every race there was a moment when the burst was least expected. The only problem was to decide the moment.

I have found that the whole race often depends on this factor. In my later races—against Landy for instance —I always bore this advice in mind. An opponent is usually least prepared to be overtaken at the beginning or just at the end of the straight, and it is often possible to gain a few precious yards by this use of surprise.

Festivities were held in check until the day of our match with Princeton and Cornell. Then each "class" in its distinctive outfit, with wives, children and hangers-on, assembled in front of the Nassau Tavern. The "P-rade" (Princeton parade) was starting. The younger classes carried banners proclaiming their exploits in the field of baby production, while the older provided the more spectacular and expensive entertainment. The procession was enlivened by brass and jazz bands, and by alumni happily gum chewing as they marched along. One class provided a troupe of performing elephants, in University colours of course.

The procession slowly made its way to the field where the annual Princeton-Yale baseball game was to take place. The "pitchers" were already warming up. After leading the "circus" once round the field the class of '24, now having their 25th reunion, released their orange gas-filled balloons. The "tiny tots" or "thirsty-firsters," so called because due to graduate in 1951, came last in the motley procession, wearing orange breeches and sucking babies' feeding bottles.

The full force of the "P-rade" on a hot sticky June day flattened us. We parted company with the alumni for a time and rested on our bunks, hoping to recover some strength and nervous energy for our own races later that afternoon.

On 11th June at Princeton, under the watchful eyes of Jack Lovelock, I ran against Ron Wittreich, the Princeton captain. My time was 4 min. 11.1 sec., the second fastest mile in America that year. Wooderson had done 4 min. 12.7 sec. in 1935 at the same age of 20, so I was keeping pace with his schedule. And, because I was already looking well ahead, I was even more pleased to find that I had reached my peak of fitness as I had planned—a peak which I felt I could now time almost to a day.

Later that night Princeton had three excuses for celebration—the baseball game, the track meet and the end of the reunion. The campus was still reeling when we left next morning.

In the middle of the following week at Yale I ran a test ¾ mile quite easily in 3 min. 6 sec., which made a mile in 4 min. 8 sec. seem possible. We stayed there in one wing of the gymnasium, christened the "cathedral of muscle." We had never before seen such facilities for sport. The athlete did not have to think, or do anything for himself—he just provided a willing obedient body, which his university clothed in athletic dress. He had only to follow his coach's instructions. Just in case he broke down under the strain the university had four whole-time psychiatrists to help undergraduates with their problems.

When we reached Harvard, their Finnish coach, kindly white-haired Iako Mijkola, was delighted to meet athletes with the European approach. He spent almost as much time coaching us as his own team. He seemed lost in the American drive for results, which, even at Harvard, turned sport into a machine in which the athlete's individuality was submerged. Iako took away my spikes on the morning of the race, grinding them as

93

sharp as needle points. He also rubbed graphite into the soles of the shoes so that none of the cinders would stick. Afterwards I always did this before an important race or record attempt. These precautions may make no difference, but in those last hours before a race I always imagine I must not neglect any assistance, however slight.

George Wade of Yale, my rival in the Yale-Harvard match, was one of the best American milers of that time. I always feel anxious, even uncomfortable, when I meet an opponent for the first time. I find it almost impossible to relax, because the fierceness that I shall need for the race rises unbidden inside me. My anxiety was greater than usual when I first saw Wade. It was the first time I had been confronted with someone of my own height, weight and physique. I had the uncanny feeling that I should be running against my own shadow, or mirror image.

My physique had changed from school days. It just happened that by now my build, with a stronger body on long legs, was almost ideal for middle-distance running. So I had more reason to fear running against my "double." I won the race on 20th June 1949 in 4 min. 11.9 sec. I might not have defeated Wade if he had not flown to Los Angeles the previous week for the American championships—perhaps he had not completely recovered. Soon after the race at Harvard he returned to his home in the Middle West where he intended to marry and settle down. This was a severe loss to American sport.

His was the attitude of many American athletes. The college system seemed to have destroyed much of the pleasure he probably found in his earlier running. During his four years at Yale he had been rushed around the States with his college team, to compete in out-door and indoor track meets. Sprinters may thrive on this treatment but it is more than most middle distance runners can stand. It destroys the freshness and sparkle which are so essential.

For several weeks after the tour was over I remained in America, staying with relatives and friends in New York. Life was a gay whirlwind of parties that soon began to pall. It seemed too much the shadow and not the substance of life. The insecurity I sensed in so many people I met transferred itself to me. In need of a rest I sought peace on Long Island, but found instead a greater unreality—a struggle to live in an endless round of pleasure. There were exclusive country clubs, parties on yachts and débutante dances. I went to a wedding in a pretty imitation of an English village church, which seemed out of keeping with this atmosphere of extravagance and luxury.

New York and Long Island are so different from the rest of America that I wanted to travel farther afield. I grew frustrated at being taken everywhere by car—it seems quite impossible to walk in America. On occasions I acquired a reputation for madness by asking for the car to be stopped and insisting on walking. I made my way North, and after staying in Albany for a week

95

took a boat home from Quebec. I landed in England on 16th July 1949, the day when Bill Nankeville won his second A.A.A. mile championship with the fastest time in the world that year—4 min. 8.8 sec.

I had taken no exercise in America for nearly six weeks and had kept very irregular hours. I hoped it would not be necessary for me to run again that year. But almost as soon as I arrived home I was told that owing to the widespread interest in my American races, there would be disappointment if I did not appear on the track in England. I agreed very reluctantly to run a half-mile in the London-Gothenburg match, on 6th August 1949. At that time I was not accustomed to this distance, and so the defeat which I expected as a result of my unfitness would be easier to bear. I arrived at the White City Stadium just before 2 o'clock, to be greeted by a worried looking team manager.

"Look here, old chap," he said, "I'm afraid I've got to ask you a favour. Morris has dropped out of the mile, and the Swedes have brought over Landqvist, their best miler. We cannot disappoint everyone—we must put up an athlete of the same class to race against him. Will you transfer to the mile?"

Quite apart from my lack of training, I had only just finished my lunch. I knew there was a good chance of getting "stitch" if I ran in the mile, which was an hour earlier than the half-mile. But I felt I could only agree.

It was a rough race—both Carlsson of Sweden and I had our legs torn by running shoes. When I am fit, my

96

ʳunning feels effortless until I start the finishing burst. But this time there was no life or joy in my running, and the agony was unbearable. My legs ached with every stride, just as they had two years before, when I had raced after the Hunt Ball. An athlete has no right to run if he is not fit—even though he may be to blame for having stopped his training. I could not raise a challenge and crawled home in third place. The race was won by Landqvist in 4 min. 12.8 sec. This was the first race in my life in which I had so decidedly failed to do what was expected of me. I felt very humbled. My time was 4 min. 14.2 sec.

As I had run when unfit, in a race I had not expected, I hoped no one would take my defeat too seriously. But as I left the Stadium the news of my defeat was already headlined in the evening papers—"Bannister fails in Mile"—"Bannister beaten into Third Place." I felt some of the chagrin of defeat as I read these words.

Every athlete and sportsman realises sooner or later the uncertainty of how the Press will react, and that he has to become indifferent to praise or censure. One can hardly expect special sympathy or understanding from critics, especially if they have never been athletes. They must find it difficult to resist pressure to make sensational headlines. It is the first blow that hurts most. In contrast I enjoyed the comments of one kindly correspondent with a sense of humour, who described my race as "an admirably controlled effort," on what he euphemistically referred to as my "light preparation."

97

At the dinner on the evening of the match I had second thoughts, and forgot my disappointment. The amazing discovery of the afternoon was that I had taken no exercise for two months and could still run a mile only three seconds slower than my best time. What price training? It does make first-class performances more easily possible and less painful. After this experience I felt that no athlete is justified in running when inadequately trained.

I decided I needed a holiday in Ireland. As soon as I landed in Dublin a man picked up my suitcase. When I made a move to pay him he said, "Sure and what would I be doing charging a handsome fellow like yourself, and you with all the Olympic glory of Zeus, and the Gods of Ancient Greece on your jacket"—I wore an Olympic blazer from the 1948 Games. "If I were to charge you, and heaven forbid that I should, 'twould only be three pence. Why don't you make it a shilling?" he grinned.

I was so glad to be among such lovable rascals that I paid up cheerfully. As I drove to my hotel the cabby had his little daughter sitting beside him, and she leaned half upside down across his lap looking out of the window.

"And tell the fine gentleman what you can see, my pretty one," he said.

She could not have been more than eight—but she piped up, "Sure, I can see the world afloatin' in space with the houses and trees growing out of the clouds.

98

Daddy I think I'm in an aeroplane." What a place for a holiday!

From the window of my hotel I could see some workmen repairing one end of Grafton Street. Some hundred yards down the road was a boiler used for heating the tar and pitch. It looked like Stephenson's "Rocket." Through the pall of thick black smoke that poured from it I could see a man draining off the molten pitch into square wooden buckets and loading them on a pony cart. The aged driver sat huddled over the reins until he had a load sufficient to cover a few square yards of road surface. Then he whipped up his decrepit pony, a mere bag of bones, and as though leading the charge of the Light Brigade, clattered down Grafton Street with his steaming load. When he reached the site of operations two men unloaded the buckets, tipping the pitch on the road surface while two others patted it into place with wooden rolling pins. So this six man team was resurfacing Grafton Street, the Regent Street of Dublin.

The Clonliffe Harriers Meeting was a carnival of sport, gay and disorganised. Cyclists, who had frequent spills, shared the grass track with runners and jumpers. The Atmosphere reminded me of the story of Trinity College's best golfer, who forced his College to redeem his pawned golf clubs whenever they wanted him to win a match. There were two 880-yards handicap races—in the first I came fifth in 1 min. 56.2 sec., and Arthur Wint won the second in 1 min. 54.8 sec., both of us from scratch position.

99

This was my first experience of a handicap race. From scratch it was depressing to see a crowd of runners of assorted ages and sizes stretched out in front all round the track. As the track was almost circular, I found myself running wide all the time to overtake the stragglers. At first I seemed to make little impression on the large bunch of runners ahead of me. As the second lap began the bunch suddenly tired, overtaxed no doubt by the energy they had expended in their brief moment of glory in the lead. I caught many of them, but round each bend there always seemed to be still more ahead. At last there was only a small group of four in front. These had either excelled themselves or been fortunate in their handicap, and they romped home ahead of me.

Handicap races are perhaps necessary when runners differ greatly in standard. But accurate timing is difficult, and such races are fortunately becoming rare in first-class competition.

That evening I went to the Abbey Theatre, which was reported to have turned down some time before a substantial cash offer to rebuild—preferring the ancient charm of its setting among tumbledown mews and slums near the Liffey. I saw an epic of the "time of the troubles" which can only rightly be seen in Dublin—*The Plough and the Stars*. I asked myself why every Irish phrase has a link with the heavens. Why did even their pennies bear harps?

Afterwards I met men in the pubs near by who were developing a new theme about leading the Army into

100

the North, and who fortified their courage nightly, propped against the bar.

Next day I escaped into the country along lanes lined with thatched cottages built of white-washed stones. A grandmother sat outside one with hens pecking the ground at her feet. A black shawl almost dating back to the Famine was flung over her shoulders. Innumerable children appeared from the small door; one could only guess at the overcrowding within.

I drove out into the strange emerald beauty of the Wicklow country—much of the land of untouched fertility. Lakes, woods and streams, like St. Kevin's cave, seemed ensheathed in the mystery of a millennium of folk lore. Yes, it was just the place for a holiday!

# CHAPTER EIGHT

# HESITATION
# AND TRANSITION
## 1949-1950

*"Still as they run they look behind,*
*They hear a voice in every wind,*
*And snatch a fearful joy."*
GRAY, ODE ON A DISTANT PROSPECT OF ETON COLLEGE.

EACH AUTUMN I looked forward to running through the countryside again after a hectic Summer on the track. But the cross-country season was always rudely interrupted at the end of November by the Oxford and Cambridge relays, for which at least a few weeks of track preparation were necessary.

In December 1949 I was included in the Oxford cross-country team for the race against Cambridge over Roehampton Common. The 7½-mile course crosses several V-shaped valleys. At first you freewheel down one side until the uphill slope on the opposite side brings you under control before you are sent sprawling. After wading through the flooded Beverley Brook more and more mud stuck to my shoes, legs, vest and shorts, until I felt I was carrying half the Common round with me.

But our Cambridge opponents were running very

strongly. Just when I was almost bogged in the "Slough of Despond," I commented with forced cheerfulness to an opponent, "I like mud, it makes the course more interesting, doesn't it?" Such unexpected heartiness evidently discouraged him, and he fell right back.

After two more miles came the long climb up the "Toast-rack." I contrived to come up to a Cambridge man, and as we reached the top I dragged myself past him with my last reserves of energy, saying as I did so, "Well, that didn't seem as bad as last year!" On this discouragement he too suddenly dropped back, and I managed somehow to reach the finish in first place in 41 min. 54 sec., the fastest time for this course since 1922.

Sometimes I think it is a pity that it is not possible to improve the situation in track races by appropriate comments between the runners. There is a happy social atmosphere about cross-country running not found on the track, connected partly with the cheerful confusion of improvised changing rooms and partly in sharing together the ups and downs of the cross-country course. I shall want to continue cross-country running when my track days are over.

My training was very light, if not inadequate, at this time. My earliest system in Oxford was to train four days a week, alternating slow runs of 1¼ miles with faster runs of ½-¾ miles, and to run a fast time trial of ¾ mile a few days before the race.

103

This method has several disadvantages. So much running on the track became boring, and I lost the sense of freshness which comes from putting on spikes only for an important race. Further, this method did not strengthen me—it merely kept me in running condition. Provided however I did not race too often I was able to run races near my best times, but without showing any decided improvement.

I ran almost entirely on nervous energy summoned for the occasion, and I needed time afterwards to recover. The night after my races I was too tired physically and too excited mentally to sleep. The muscles of my legs would ache. Large quantities of salt are lost through excessive perspiration, and if I did not eat salt immediately after the race I was wracked with cramp.

Then Jim Alford, A.A.A. coach, lent me an account of the training methods of Gunder Haegg, the Swedish world record holder for the mile. Haegg used a method called *fartlek*, meaning speed-play, in which he ran almost entirely on grass. He alternated gentle running with fast running over distances from 100 yards to a mile. The aim is to give speed and stamina to the athlete, imitating the games involving short bursts of running and recovering which children play. I began to modify my methods along these lines, and this principle has formed the basis of my subsequent training.

On 18th March 1950 I lowered the inter-Varsity record again with a 4 min. 14.8 sec. mile. This was my fourth consecutive victory, and my last opportunity of competing in this event.

In my college we had stumbled across the happy information that Exeter College Athletic Club was about the oldest in the country, having been founded in 1850. This fact seemed to deserve a centenary celebration.

Considering what we know about the diet of the athletes of those days, it seems remarkable that any running at all was possible. We could not follow them in their dietary fads of underdone steak with liberal quantities of beer and port wine. We contented ourselves with a meeting run on 1850 lines.

Besides the usual events we included consolation stakes over 300 yards, and obstacle races, but we had unfortunately to draw the line at donkey races. Everyone ran in gym shoes, and some had the additional handicap of side whiskers and top hats, which added considerably to their discomfort, not to mention the increased wind resistance. As I was handicapped hopelessly in the half-mile, I had to win the 100 yards in order to secure one of the highly prized centenary medals, struck specially for the occasion. As a description in a journal of the 1850's would have ended, "there were many ladies present."

At this time I was working for my Oxford medical exams and had little time for training. I found running in moderation helped my work, but hard training was strong meat to be indulged in only sparingly. When the

105

exams arrived, I suspect I unwittingly transferred my knack of releasing nervous energy on the running track to the less appropriate site of the examination hall, with undesirable if not harmful results. At times I reduced myself to a nervous panic.

On 1st July 1950, the day after my exams, I ran a 4 min. 13 sec. mile against the American Universities at the White City Stadium, with a last lap in 57.5 sec., my fastest time in England up to that date. The American team of 19 athletes was accompanied by 11 officials.

The next day I travelled to Finland with David Dixon and Nick Stacey, who had followed me in turn as President of the Oxford University Athletic Club.

They were a contrast in personalities. David Dixon was perhaps more serious-minded than many of my Oxford contemporaries. He returned to Lincoln College after a period of air-crew service in the R.A.F., and although he hurdled successfully in University and open competition, athletics meant perhaps less to him than to other members of the team. He was already preparing for his legal career, and left Oxford with a first-class degree. He has since spent a year at Harvard Law School on a Commonwealth Fund Fellowship.

Nick Stacey was cheerful and unpredictable. At first I found it difficult to reconcile his apparent irresponsibility with his avowed intention of entering the Church. After his education at Dartmouth, Nick had been a regular Naval Officer, but had left the Service to prepare

106

for the Ministry. Later I realised that he is a man of surprising contrasts. He would leave at the end of a particularly rowdy Oxford party and go out to North Oxford to visit a group of children to whom he acted as a guardian. His vacation time was divided between international athletic competition and periods of social service work. The one could never be deduced from the other, and his apparent cynicism was a mask for a deep sense of religious and social purpose. Nick retired from active athletics after reaching the semi-final of the 200 metres at Helsinki. He now regards his athletics experience of importance only if it helps him to make contact with young people and to show them the living reality of Christian faith.

I already had a special interest in Finland, where the Olympic Games were to be held two years later. Three was an ideal number for a tour of this kind. We were invited by the Helsinki University Club as a gesture of friendliness towards Oxford, and hired out like circus performers to local athletic clubs for track meetings, in order to cover our travel expenses. We travelled hundreds of miles through forest land haunted by the mood of Sibelius, to the tundra and perpetual daylight of far-off Lapland.

Finland had just completed payment of her reparations to Russia, and was fiercely independent, anxious to show that her affinities were with the West rather than the East. I remember watching Finnish lumber women

107

wielding long sticks with metal spikes on the ends. They sat perched in empty oil canisters moored to buoys in the estuary. As the timber logs floated by, they would identify those belonging to the different timber companies and direct them into the correct channels.

Some American world record holders were touring Finland at the same time, and we were naturally not anxious to compete against them too often. All went well until Dick Attesley, who had recently broken the world record for the high hurdles, crossed our path. He finished a race of 110 metres hurdles in his world record time of 13.5 sec. before David had cleared the last hurdle. This margin was too much for David, who retired on the spot. He had not bargained for competition of this calibre in a Finnish village of a few hundred inhabitants.

In Finland the spectators are better educated, athletically, than anywhere else in the world. They do not merely gaze at the spectacle but are critical of the standard of performance, and points of technique and style. They reserve their applause so that they do not debase its currency. They know that the interest and pleasure to be derived from athletics are cumulative; the more they know about it the more intense is their critical enjoyment.

On my return from Finland I decided to run nothing but half-miles. As I had been unable to train in the early season I knew that I could not expect to run well. Half-miles would be less of a strain and would give me valuable tactical experience in coping with a large field of runners moving considerably faster than in mile races. Tactical errors, such as lying fourth on the last bend, which can be rectified in a mile race, may be fatal in a half mile; one's thinking must be so much quicker. I also wanted to develop my speed. At the same time I decided not to take my running too seriously—to enjoy it and to postpone my long term plans.

In the A.A.A. championships on 15th July 1950, I ran my first half mile against Arthur Wint, the Olympic 400 metres champion. It was like leaning out from our respective events above and below this distance to shake hands with each other. We were good friends. Only on one occasion was I able to make a serious challenge.

I had a strange feeling in running behind him. He was 6 ft. 5 in., with legs long in proportion even for this height. His length of stride was so great that it interfered with the natural rhythm of my own running. Arthur Wint was the only runner I had met who could influence my length of stride. He dominated me so much that I almost wished I could fit in two strides to his one. I had to keep at a respectful distance—it was like running against a giant.

He is the greatest natural athlete I have seen, with fine muscular and chest development and a graceful stride without any sign of tension. His great charm endeared him to fellow athletes and spectators alike. I am told

109

that when I or any other English half milers were running behind him we looked like little boys chasing our
big uncle. Sometimes he looked ungainly when he ran,
like a big man attempting to run slowly. He relied
mainly on his natural ability, not training as much as
half milers today. In the A.A.A. championship half
mile of 1950 Wint beat me with ease in 1 min. 51.6 sec.,
though I ran my fastest time of 1 min. 52.1 sec., with a
good burst over the last 250 yards.

Next day I flew to Greece with an Achilles team.
Since the 1948 Games I had been impatient to visit the
home of ancient athletics and to see for myself Olympia,
Marathon and the modern Greek Stadium in Athens.
This Stadium was built for the first modern Games in
1896 on the site of the original Stadium. The track is
narrow and extremely long (180 yards—1 stade, the nearest ancient Greek equivalent to our 100 yards sprint)
with sharp bends at each end to make the total circuit
440 yards. The stands were built of white marble, and
gleamed in floodlights which were outshone as the full
moon rose in the Mediterranean sky. The Greeks themselves seemed to have little of the athletic ability of their
ancestors. They scored mainly in their expertness in
negotiating the sharp bends. Where an Achilles runner
was forced to run wide to prevent himself over-balancing,
a Greek would overtake him on the inside and emerge
into the next straight some yards in the lead.

We dined outdoors on the Piræus waterfront, eating

110

fried octopus and drinking retzina wine. We watched Greek sailors dancing, and gazed at the lanterns swinging astern the midnight fishing boats

When I returned to England Wint again beat me over 880 yards in the international triangular match at the White City on 7th August 1950. I came up to Wint's shoulder on the last back straight, but he forged ahead to win easily in 1 min. 52.4 sec.—my time was 1 min. 54.5 sec.

On the following Saturday in a half mile at the White City, Mal Whitfield (U.S.A.) showed that Wint was not invincible. Whitfield's bounding uneconomical stride carried him well ahead with half a lap to go. Wint was unable to sprint in the last stages of a race run in this way. He could hardly control his vast length of leg. He cracked in the finishing straight when he started to shrug his shoulders as he ran.

My first taste of full international competition came in the Final of the European Games 800 metres in Brussels on 26th August 1950. I was ill prepared for such an important race. John Parlett, who ran a 1 min. 50.9 sec. 800 metres in the Olympic semi-final at Wembley in 1948, was the other British representative. Our opponents included Audun Boysen, the young Norwegian, who had startled the world some weeks before with a 1 min. 48.7 sec. 800 metres. There were also Marcel Hansenne of France, who took third place in the Olympic 800 metres Final of 1948 at Wembley, and Jose

111

Barthel of Luxembourg, later Olympic 1,500 metres champion at Helsinki in 1952.

This was my first international "scrambling" race. Boysen rushed into the lead with a suicidal first lap of 50.9 sec. I lay fourth in 53.8 sec., a time which I could barely have returned for a 440 yards race. The jostling took me quite by surprise, and I found myself in the middle of the runners with elbows pushing me on all sides. After moving up on the back straight I held the lead round the last bend and into the finishing straight. Then Parlett came alongside and edged past me as if blown along by a private gust of wind. Thirty yards from the tape I had no strength left. Somehow I staggered on—taking an overdraft from some hidden source. Just as I tottered over the line Marcel Hansenne came up on the outside. Parlett had won by a foot in 1 min. 50.5 sec., and I was declared second. There was an appeal. The jury met, the photo finish was examined and Hansenne was given the second place, with the same time for each of us of 1 min. 50.7 sec.

After this I decided that it was not tactical sense I lacked. I had survived the elbow battle and had reached a winning position. The situation in each race is different, and it is a question of thinking quickly enough. I doubt if this ability is improved much by practice. I simply lacked the strength to make use of a good position. This strength could only come from consistent training. After this meeting I began to realise the strain

112

of international competition and the greater intensity of nervousness it produced. University matches had been crippling enough but this was ten times worse.

On my return from Brussels, Parlett beat me at Edinburgh in a slow half mile of 2 min. 3.6 sec., and also in a match against France in Paris on 9th September, when his time was 1 min. 53.5 sec. for 800 metres. I won an end of the season race of 800 metres against him in Gothenburg, when we returned the same time of 1 min. 53.1 sec.

Since July I had been beaten in five major races—though I had enjoyed them all. I was beginning to think it did not matter if I was beaten. This would have been fatal to my future as a runner. Until this year there had been the stimulus that no one had beaten me in an important race. Now it had happened so often that I was becoming almost happy-go-lucky. I had completed an experiment in racing. I drew the conclusion that although I could run fast times on inadequate training, I could not be sure of winning.

For two months I had been competing in athletic meetings in six different countries of Europe. Apart from Finland and Greece, I saw very little of the countries I visited, and with each fresh journey my sense of frustration had grown. I might just as well have run all my races at the White City in London.

I had flown from capital to capital. My suitcases were covered with the labels of expensive hotels, in which

I could not have afforded to stay myself, nor would I have wanted to; but hotels like these were my racing headquarters. I should have preferred climbing mountains abroad, but this was out of the question. The risk of a sprained ankle was too great.

Waiters swept by me with exotic dishes that might tickle the palate even if later they upset the stomach. Dishes with names that roll off the tongue, like scalopini, zabaglioni, ravioli, were not for me, nor the wines that keep them company. I ended my simple meal with a glass of milk. It was only a matter of time before mental boredom set in.

One day I found myself in Paris—half way up the Eiffel Tower in a lift like a bird cage. I was hemmed in, so it seemed to me, by women with feathery hats clutching guide books. As the lift went up I had the odd feeling that precedes a crisis. Aggressive thoughts began to chase across my mind. I felt I knew every conversation around me before it began. We all seemed so self-conscious, rambling round Paris in hordes. I knew I was being unreasonable but I could not prevent myself looking fierce so that I would be left alone. I felt I was out of sympathy with other people. This was the danger signal. I had to escape from it all.

There and then I decided what to do. The Eiffel Tower is just the place in which to have a crisis and to make a decision. I did not trouble to look out at the top. I took the next lift down the tower, whistling cheer-

114

fully as we shot back to earth. With a light heart that had been missing from my running for some time, I returned to my hotel and cancelled my reservation. How cheaply I bought my freedom!

I left a note for my friends and strode into the nearest shoe shop. I bought a heavy pair of walking boots. Their clanging on the pavement made everyone stare. I had never hitch-hiked before but I was certain this was the moment to begin. In rusty schoolboy French I tried to find a car or lorry that would take me south, but no one seemed to understand what I was talking about.

It might not be as easy as I had expected. Perhaps it was impossible to start hitching until I had shaken the dust of the city from my feet and was well outside Paris. As I waited for a train I bought a kilo of grapes and sat with my feet dangling over a bridge. I munched the grapes and spat the pits on the line with great precision, dreaming about lifts on lorries. Then a train arrived and took me on the first stage of my journey.

I found that hitch-hiking was a little like bathing in cold water. It is the first plunge that is frightening. But I was soon enjoying every minute of it and gaining confidence. I wandered across the south of France, hitching lifts as I went. I followed the river Rhone into Switzerland.

A hitcher does not get something for nothing. He makes a positive contribution which the driver appreciates. In his own small way he knocks down international

115

barriers, making friends where conventional tourists never venture. He is welcomed as the only kind of tourist who gives his ideas instead of his money—perhaps in backwaters of the countryside where war and American films are the only uncomfortable reminders that other ways of life exist. A hitcher is not without honour except in his own country.

From the Rhone Glacier in Switzerland I crossed the St. Gothard Pass into Italy. I could have spent days watching the warm wind from Lake Lugano swirling autumn leaves round the town squares, but the hitcher gets impatient for fresh people and places. I never refused any lift that was offered me. The subtlest delight in hitching is that you never quite reach the destination you intended. But what does that matter? You have a good friend in the driver. He is always very anxious about you, and envious of your freedom. He suddenly realises that his car is a burden, dragging him mercilessly from this place to that. He isn't lucky enough to spend some nights on lorries, some in fields, some in barns. He cannot escape for long enough to sun-bathe within sight of the snows of Monte Rosa.

On one occasion I was trying to get to Lyons. An old truck rattled to a stop beside me. I was suspicious of the driver's keenness that I should join him, but thought no more about it and climbed into the cabin. The lorry refused to start. The driver looked at me dubiously as if I were the culprit and climbed out to crank the engine.

I got out too, and it was then that I caught my first full view of the lorry. There had been so many adaptations and repairs that all traces of the original outline were lost. The wheels had an air of detachment. The chassis rode above them with arresting vertical lines, and its sides were hidden by two enormous galvanised objects, which might have been anything from bedsteads to baking stoves. The situation seemed hopeless.

"I might be asked to push the wretched thing," I thought in despair. Now that I had accepted the lift I was a partner in the driver's misfortune. It was not long indeed before I was pushing the lorry, because cranking was useless. It was lucky the lorry was filled with empty tins and junk, and that the brow of a hill was only 30 yards away. As we began to roll down the other side the engine picked up on three cylinders. With a shattering noise we were off!

Nothing seemed to disturb the driver's perpetual smile, not even the prospect of spending a perishing September night somewhere along the road to Lyons. Sadly the lorry slowed down and with a dying gasp shuddered to a halt. Somehow we started it again, each bolt and screw groaning as we toiled up the hills. But we always sped down the other side joyously, farmers and villagers coming out to stare at the rattling junk, with me perched aloft.

A hitch-hiker is not always lucky. There are moments when he thinks he will never get a lift, but something

117

always turns up. When I am working in hospital or walking through a London fog, I look back on that holiday as one thinks of summer when snow is on the ground.

# CHAPTER NINE

# TRAINING AND TOURING

## 1950-1951

*"Youth is the time to go flashing from one
end of the world to the other."*
R. L. STEVENSON, VIRGINIBUS PUERISQUE.

IT WAS AUTUMN OF 1950 and two years before the next
Olympic Games in Helsinki. I worked out a plan which
would, I hoped, bring me to a peak for the great race.
Having stepped up my training programme, I would
run in as many first-class meetings as possible during the
year. I intended also to travel widely in many countries
so that I could get used to changes of food and climate.
I also hoped to meet most of the opponents I was likely
to race against in Helsinki. This would help me to find
out their special points, and if possible their weak spots.

After a year of this, my Olympic preparation would begin in earnest. I would not leave England and would
rely on training rather than racing. I hoped this would
give me strength without draining my nervous energy.

I spent my time in England doing some research in
Oxford on the factors responsible for the increase in
breathing during exercise. Having taken my degree at

Exeter College I was appointed to a research scholarship at Merton, which carried some dining rights at High Table. For a year I lived in a world intermediate between undergraduate and fellow—between earth and heaven. I was supervised in my research by Prof. C. G. Douglas, F.R.S., and worked in close co-operation with Dr. D. J. C. Cunningham. The physiological problem I tackled was entirely academic, unlikely to shed any light on the practical problems of running and training. I spent nearly all my time in the laboratory, conducting experiments in which subjects breathing different gas mixtures ran on a motor-driven treadmill at different speeds and gradients. My real work began when the run on the treadmill was over and I had to make endless gas analyses, attempting to sort out the factors controlling breathing during exercise.

Gradually I began to understand the infinite capacity for taking pains that is necessary before any scientific advance can be made. The discipline of research is exacting and gruelling. Each experiment, even though it may be only one in a series of hundreds, must be considered of vital significance in itself. It may prove to be the experiment producing a variation which explodes one's preconceptions—even the most careful inductive scientist allows himself the luxury of some preliminary general speculation.

In the laboratory my own untidy nature was gradually curbed as I tried to capture some of the exactitude of the scientific method. Yet as my work became more accurate, my personal tidiness, never very noticeable, degenerated, as though by some law of compensation. Clothing and meals were neglected in the excitement of possible discoveries. I invariably lost letters or mislaid odd socks, and never seemed to have time to organise my domestic front.

One morning, dressing hurriedly to catch a train, I lost sight of my collar and wandered round the house searching for this vital piece of clothing. I grew desperate, with visions of a missed train, appointments not kept, and personal disaster. Finally I was persuaded to make a methodical search, and discovered the collar inside my shirt, resting under my arm-pit.

For a short period one can live in an untidy personal world, but once inside the laboratory I tried to be more accurate and careful, so that I did not waste the value of work already done.

Some of this objectivity and care was carried over into my running. I began to prepare my training programme and to test my physical reactions with the same precision that I had learnt in the laboratory.

Quite apart from my own research problem I grew interested in medical problems related to running in general rather than my own running in particular. I started from the physical stand-point, wondering why some men are able to become athletes and some are not. Training is important, but not everyone gets the same benefit from it. Can a doctor select those who are capable of becoming athletes?

121

An early attempt to classify physique was made over 2,000 years ago by Hippocrates, who described two basic physiques—habitus phthisicus and habitus apoplecticus —the extreme thin man and the extreme fat man. A similar principle is used today, though Sheldon has added a third extreme—the mesomorphic or muscular man. It seems that athletes tend to have a physique high in the factors of thinness and muscularity.

From a small group of Oxford athletes it was not possible to correlate superlative athletic ability with particular physical characteristics. Such studies only confirmed the less scientific observations of coaches and trainers who select a man for a particular event by "eye."

There are obvious exceptions to the normal concepts of what a runner's build should be. Chataway, for example, has a strength and power in his chest and shoulders that tempt one to suggest that he would be more at home in the boxing ring than on the running track. Yet his potential as a three-miler is as great as any athlete's in the world. Physique is only one of many factors.

Other physical methods for selecting athletes have been suggested, but these are as yet somewhat empirical. One idea is that by using a formula based on height, weight and heart size, it may be possible to choose the people who would make outstanding athletes, but it is unlikely that such formulæ would be effective in practice.

Luckily it is still much more reliable to judge from seeing a man run or jump than it is to test his potentialities in a laboratory. If a laboratory forecast were

122

possible there would be hardly any point in an athlete's proving his ability, and he would never experience the satisfaction of struggle and achievement. I hope the frightening day will never come when the scientist can predict with accuracy the limits of an athlete's success.

It is just as difficult for a doctor to assess an athlete's potential from a clinical examination at rest. Athletes usually have low pulse rates. My own is 40 to 50 at rest, compared with an average of 70, but this is mainly the result of athletic training. It probably only indicates that an athlete's efficient heart and lungs can cope with the normal requirements of the body at rest much more easily than those of a normal person.

Sometimes an athlete's pulse at rest may have minor irregularities. A case is known of a world record holder who fainted in the course of an ordinary medical examination. The key to this paradox is found when the athlete begins to exercise. Far from being a sick man he quickly passes to a state of extreme efficiency. His integration of heart and lungs may be more efficient when he is running at ten miles an hour than when he is sitting in an arm chair. This is perhaps as striking a tribute to the body's philosophy, which seems to prefer movement, as to its physiology, which makes this movement possible. The waddling gait and breathlessness of a muscle-bound weight-lifter are salutary warnings of the dangers of over-specialization, and of what occurs when muscular development has been carried to excess. The middle

123

distance runner does not increase the bulk of his muscles, but he does increase their efficiency.

At Christmas 1950 I travelled out to the Centennial Games in New Zealand with Arthur Wint and Emmanuel McDonald Bailey, with the additional duties of team manager. McDonald Bailey, like Wint, was a West Indian athlete, and the pair dominated British sprinting and middle distance running between 1946 and 1952. McDonald Bailey had perhaps the most consistently successful record of any modern sprinter, and his career was crowned by his world record run of 10.2 seconds for the 100 metres at Zagreb in 1951. They were both about 10 years older than I and much more experienced athletes.

My natural wanderlust was more satisfied by this tour than by any other I have made. In my mind I had a model framework of the world dating from my rudimentary knowledge of geography learnt as a child. I was impatient to fill in the blanks with real images and pictures from my own experiences.

The flight to New Zealand provided much greater interest than did my crossing to America. We flew over the snow-capped Alps and circled Vesuvius on our way to Egypt. We saw the pyramids in the twilight, and the sunbaked city of Cairo looking quite fresh in the early morning air. As we crossed India the channels of the Ganges delta looked like the crooked fingers of witches pointed warningly against invaders.

124

We stayed one night in Singapore. Cars were up-turned in the street—the result of riots over the future of a Dutch girl brought up by Malayan foster parents. The sights and sounds of an eastern city, the crowded streets and babble, are too much to be taken in on a first visit. We spent the next night in the tropical humidity of northern Australia at Darwin, in huts built on piles to guard against the ravages of the white ant.

Four days of continuous flying coupled with sight-seeing when we should have been sleeping had brought us to a stupor of fatigue. Sydney Bridge, ranked as one of the wonders of the modern world, raised barely a murmur of excitement in us, and the little we saw of the city itself spelt brashness and Coca-Cola to our insensi-tive minds. We spent an hour or so watching the Test Match in Sydney in an alert and noisy atmosphere that contrasted rudely with the stolid respectability of Lord's. Our curiosity was temporarily satiated, and we were im-patient to complete the last stage of our journey.

With other Centennial Game visitors we flew across the Southern Alps of New Zealand to land in Christ-church a week after leaving London. We emerged from 24 hours' deep sleep to find ourselves in a Presbyterian School—we might easily have been in the British Isles. The native redwood interior echoed some of the stern austerity and renunciation of a Scottish Sunday.

It was mid-summer in New Zealand. Soon we were eating our Christmas dinner and sunning ourselves by the stream that lazed through the grounds of the school.

125

Weeping willows along its banks looked like strands of green velvet against a background of copper beeches. The school itself groaned with Victorian elaborations— winding staircases, sloping roofs, turrets and verandahs.

The celebration in which we were taking part was much more than a sporting event; it was to commemorate the centenary of the settlement of Canterbury Plain in New Zealand. It was exactly a hundred years since their first ships sailed into Lyttleton Harbour—four months after these courageous adventurers left England.

While we were there, the New Zealanders were reenacting the landing of 1850, in which a cross-section of the England that was being changed by the Industrial Revolution was shipped lock, stock and barrel to New Zealand. The original planners transferred clergyman, doctor and schoolteacher, farmer and labourer, in the right proportions, thinking to make a stable society. They hoped to barricade themselves against the leaven of social change that had already overtaken England.

Now their descendants were again slowly climbing the range of hills separating the coast from the fertile Canterbury Plain which their ancestors had chosen. At the summit they rested by a simple stone cross on which had been carved in commemoration, "They passed by here." Looking back from the stone cross to the harbour, alongside the replicas of the early sailing ships, we saw modern freighters waiting to unload. New Zealand was crippled at the time by dock strikes. The contrast was too great. The foresight and idealism of those

126

early planners were not good enough to give them a smooth transition to a welfare state.

I won my race from a field which included Willi Slijkhuis from Holland, the European 1,500 metres champion. We ran on a grass track, and my time of 4 min. 9.9 sec. was my fastest so far. Don Macmillan, the Australian miler, who came second, confided to me afterwards, "You only become really friendly with your opponents after you've beaten them!" Perhaps this was true. I naturally eyed my rivals suspiciously, after having travelled 7,000 miles to race against them for four brief minutes.

In the anti-climax after this effort I was beaten the following day in a half-mile race. This defeat received almost as much attention as my victory in the mile race. By now I felt relatively impervious to unfavourable Press comment, which takes no account of individual temperament. I preferred to reserve myself for the important races.

We crossed the border to the "Scottish" town of Timaru, and ran as best we could to the swirling tunes of full dress pipe bands. We kept one eye on the Highland dancing girls. As with the Highland Games in Edinburgh there was too much going on at once for any single event to be taken seriously. I remember a light-hearted win against Arthur Wint in a half-mile, when we played a cat and mouse game.

Buoyed up by the Mayor's story that Mount Cook could be seen on a fine day we survived two days of merciless rain in Timaru, but had to leave without catching sight of their famous mountain.

At Timaru I saw the school where Lovelock spent his boyhood. The oak sapling awarded to Olympic victors in Berlin was growing in front of the school as an inspiration to successive generations of his countrymen. As I stood in the cold and rain of the summer I realised that a boy would need to be tough to withstand a winter in one of the school dormitories with the side walls open to the weather.

It was while spending a few days in the peaceful and prosperous sheep farming land of an isolated peninsula that I realised how much I missed England. I had rarely felt homesick before. It suddenly dawned on me that I had lived too long in towns to be able to adjust myself to the life of a farmer, with his more solid satisfaction of caring for land and animals. The residents seemed the natural descendants of the original gentlemen farmers who had almost used kid gloves to shear the sheep.

I appreciated it all but I could not share it. I was forced to admit that there were some ways of life that could never be mine. I was sad because I like to feel that I can share the pleasure of other ways of life. I missed most the stress, toil and uncertainty of England. Prosperity does not automatically lead to happiness. The agility and vigour of a people are in danger of declining when they are too free from external stresses. The mood in England that makes life exciting is the determination to build a new way of life instead of preserving an old one as the original settlers in New Zealand had hoped to do. But I was sad to leave a country with such hospitality.

We had a transitory welcome in the perpetual smiles and cheerful correctness of Fiji, and we experienced American efficiency in Honolulu, where we received tourist treatment for eight dollars head-tax—extra for garlands of flowers. I preferred America without the garlands. San Francisco and Los Angeles seemed almost like home, and Washington even more so.

We reached London again some five weeks after leaving England. The world is round after all, but somehow I still cannot understand it.

During the Spring of 1951 I continued my experiments in Oxford on the control of breathing. I grew interested in the factors leading to the point of exhaustion. It is only in sports like athletics, which are uncomplicated by "skill of eye," that men reach the last stage of exhaustion.

Energy for running comes from the breakdown of a form of sugar which is stored in the blood, liver and muscles. The breakdown is carried out most efficiently with the help of oxygen breathed from the air, less efficiently by chemical breakdown systems within the body.

The sprinter, who at full speed may be running at 25 miles-an-hour, is limited by factors independent of training. There is insufficient time to get the benefit of

129

the oxygen he breathes during a 100 yards race—he is relying on his accumulated reserves. Hence it does not matter whether or not a sprinter takes a breath during the course of such a short race.

The sprinter has to rely on the energy provided by a less efficient mechanism than the direct use of oxygen, a mechanism which results in the accumulation of progressively greater quantities of a harmful substance—lactic acid. The concentration of this acid can increase by twenty times after a sprint race, when the runner becomes breathless and dizzy. Because of his powerful physique the sprinter is well adapted to a short dash involving an extravagant burst of energy without regard to the quantity of lactic acid produced.

The sprinter's performance is not greatly improved by training, except perhaps in starting practice. The sprinter is born not made.

I am more particularly interested in middle distance running. The middle distance runner's problem is the transfer of sufficient oxygen to the muscles so that he does not have to fall back until the last stages of the race on the less efficient mechanism of energy liberation which produces lactic acid. Two systems needed to be studied—the lungs, which bring oxygen to the blood, and the circulatory system, which carries the oxygen from lung to muscle. Breathing and circulatory measurements could be made while I ran. I used the motor-driven treadmill in the laboratory on which the speed and gradient could be altered so as to exhaust the toughest athlete in a few minutes. In time I learnt to repeat my performance on the treadmill so that I could study the effect on my performance of changes in body temperature, in the acidity of the blood, and in the composition of the air breathed in. The weak link in the body which seems to prevent a man from running middle distance races faster is the failure of the supply of oxygen to the muscles. If unnecessary movements are eliminated, oxygen consumption is less and running efficiency is consequently improved. This is why running in an easy relaxed way imposes less strain without loss of speed.

In some of my experiments I used other athletes as guinea pigs; and in some, non-athletes. In one series in which the severity of the exercise was arranged so that the victims reached a breaking point after running for eight minutes when breathing atmospheric air, they appeared to be able to continue longer or almost indefinitely when breathing 66 per cent oxygen. It seems clear that if an athlete could find a practical way of breathing high concentrations of oxygen, no middle distance records would be beyond his grasp. Whether such help is justifiable in what is after all only a sport belongs to ethics rather than physiology. It is my own personal opinion that it is not justifiable.

Oxygen lack, as experienced at the end of a mile race, affects both mind and body. One victim, who suddenly began breathing 66 per cent oxygen instead of atmos-

131

pheric air, said that everything immediately looked brighter, and that he had an extraordinary sense of elation. Something very like the oxygen lack suffered by athletes happens also to mountaineers because air at high altitudes contains progressively less oxygen.

There is, for instance, the experience of Maurice Herzog, who climbed Annapurna, one of the Himalayan peaks, 26,493 ft. high, without the aid of oxygen apparatus. In his book *Annapurna* (Jonathan Cape Ltd.) he describes his descent from the peak to Camp V on 3rd June 1950. In hurrying down he became out of breath. He undid his rucksack, but immediately forgot why he had opened it.

Then he saw his gloves rolling down the slope. He was just able to realise that the consequences might be serious, and that he must rush down quickly to the camp. It never occurred to him that he was carrying socks for use as gloves in just such an emergency.

On reaching the camp, a friend, speechless with delight, clasped his hands. Suddenly his smile vanished. Herzog adds, "There was an uneasy silence. I had forgotten that I had lost my gloves: my fingers were violet and hard as wood."

Can we be surprised if runners in the last stages of exhaustion, they too suffering from lack of oxygen, do not always show their normal track sense and judgment?

I wondered then whether the challenge of Everest was so great that the assistance of oxygen was justified. This question has since been settled, but that does not mean that the same assistance is permissible for the four-minute mile.

Experiments in the laboratory are not of much practical value to athletes. There is, in fact, little scientific evidence in favour of many of the things done in training. The adaptation of the body to the stress of running is of such bewildering complexity that the athlete is forced to fall back on common sense as his practical guide. A medical training aims at increasing the power of careful observation and logical deduction. Because understanding other people starts from understanding ourselves, the self analysis which sport entails can be very helpful to the medical student.

Ever since I started running I have been trying various methods of training and racing. Each race is an experiment. There are too many factors which cannot be completely controlled for two races to be the same, just as two similar scientific experiments seldom give exactly the same results. By learning, often unconsciously, from mistakes, I discovered my reactions—both desirable and undesirable—to many of the situations I was likely to meet in big races. The athlete is essentially a wild animal who has brought himself under control except for the primitive passion unleashed in his athletic efforts.

It was my aim to minimise the effect of the undesirable factors in my running which I could not entirely eliminate, so that my running in a big race would have the spontaneous joy I felt as a boy running wildly along the shore. I wanted to remove all uncertainty and worry except the great uncertainty of victory which is the main driving force. Only in this way could my whole being become absorbed in the struggle.

# CHAPTER TEN

# BENJAMIN FRANKLIN MILE AND FIRST BRITISH TITLE

## 1951

*"Nay, if you get it you shall get it with running."*
KING LEAR.

AFTER THREE MONTHS IN ENGLAND I felt the frustration of severe training without a race to release all my pent up energy. This feeling of aggression came as a surprise to me. My outlook was quite different from that of the previous year, simply because I was stronger and faster as a result of better training. I had now definitely adopted the interval method of running, and was training about five days a week.

In 1951 I accepted an invitation to compete in April in the Benjamin Franklin Mile at the Penn Relay Meeting in Philadelphia. This was one of the biggest annual meetings in America, the Franklin Mile being a special invitation event. An Oxford don asked me just before I left, "Do tell me, how far exactly is a Benjamin Franklin mile?" Many considered that I was rash to accept

135

an invitation so early in the season without preliminary races, but on previous occasions I had found that I could reach my peak by training only.

Two weeks before leaving England, on Tuesday 18th April, I ran a ¾-mile trial at Motspur Park in 2 min. 56.8 sec. Andersson's world record stood at 2 min. 56.6 sec., so I was getting close. My lap times were 60, 59.7 and 57.1 sec., with a total time nearly 3 sec. less than Wooderson's record of 2 min. 59.6 sec., made in 1939. It was a very quiet affair—an evening meeting between Chris Chataway's club (Walton) and Imperial College. There was a last minute search for qualified time-keepers. This was the first of many occasions when Chris Chataway helped me with the pacing in the early stages. I always found it easier if I did not have to lead all the way.

I felt that I had reached world class at last. I have speculated since what would have happened if I had carried on another lap to make up the mile. After this Joe Binks was able to write that the four-minute mile could no longer be regarded as a joke, but I knew that in fact it was a very long way off. Nor was I even prepared to think about it until the great hurdle of the Olympic Games was surmounted.

The A.A.A. are normally unwilling to allow athletes to travel abroad unaccompanied, because of the many complications that may arise. I received special permission for the trip to America, on the ground that it was not solely athletic; at the University of Pennsylvania

136

Medical School I hoped to learn a technique of gas analysis not yet in use in Oxford. I was not without travel experience as I had taken the Oxford and Cambridge team to America two years earlier.

It did not occur to me that the Americans would think my lone arrival strange. I went over with two jobs to do instead of one—to me it was as simple as that. But when I stepped off the plane and was engulfed by reception committees and newspaper men, I soon realised how mistaken I was. They were amazed. Where was my manager? Where was my coach?

I felt highly embarrassed that I could not produce anyone, and at first I wished that Jack Crump, secretary of the British Amateur Athletic Board, was by my side. Gradually I got a chance to explain that I believed the athlete should coach himself as far as possible. Only he could assess his reactions to different training programmes; it was part of the fun of the sport to experiment, and if he did not win he had only himself to blame. The general Press reaction was summed up the following day by one reporter who wrote, "No manager, no trainer, no masseur, no friends! He's nuts—or he's good!"

I did not like the atmosphere of athleticism in the University training building. Even at mealtimes aggressive looking football stars glared down from portraits on the walls. So I asked to be put up at an ordinary hotel.

For a week I submitted to the ballyhoo of Press conferences, broadcasts, photographs and television interviews. Yet in spite of it all I managed to keep fairly calm. This was partly because an Englishman in America is not misled by all the ballyhoo—he begins to assess it at its true value. In particular I had a belief that I would win. This was based on the faith that my method of training and racing was the right one and that the American method was wrong. It did not cross my mind that right does not always triumph.

Both Fred Wilt and Don Gehrman, America's most consistent milers since the war, had done faster times than I. But they had also just finished a racing season on "boards" indoors in many towns in the East, and in New York at Madison Square Garden after the ballet season was over.

This was my first "mile of the century." A fourth runner, John Ray, was due to run in our race. I found an account of a race in which Ray set the early pace for Wilt. He allowed Wilt to pass him at the bell, but when Gehrman tried to follow he found his way blocked. This made me a little worried. I cast my mind back to Wooderson's visit in 1936 when he came fourth in his race. It was suggested then that the American runners Cunningham, Fenske and others boxed him in on the last bend so that he could not win. Sydney has in fact assured me that no such thing occurred. It was simply that after a week on the boat, and the great publicity, to which he was not accustomed, he was not at his best. Otherwise he could probably have won easily.

138

In the Press, Wilt and Gehrman were reported to have had a tiff. Gehrman had won ten consecutive indoor races, though Wilt was credited with the fastest time of 4 min. 5.5 sec., done on a straight stretch on Atlantic City's "boardwalk." Gehrman's tactics were always the same. He followed Wilt's pace until the finishing straight. Then, having a better "kick" he nipped past and won. These tactics were of course quite legitimate, but very aggravating to Wilt.

Before a big race a minor incident is apt to seem like a grave threat. I was training with some sprinters on the Wednesday before the Saturday of the race. I seldom sprint in normal training, but on this occasion I was eager not to appear too slow. The unusual speed left me very stiff. I spent the next two days having alternate hot and cold baths, but the stiffness remained. However, when the day of the race finally came, this trivial upset was forgotten in the excitement.

On the Saturday, 28th April 1951, there was a crowd of 40,000, which is very large for an American track meet. Track and field athletics are not normally as popular with spectators in America as in England, but the Press campaign must have had some effect. Just before the race I talked with forced confidence to Wilt and Gehrman. To me neither looked particularly happy, and this gave me hope.

For the first two laps I ran mechanically, feeling too uncertain to want to take the lead. Ray set the pace, and

139

I hesitated until the middle of the third lap when he began slowing down. Soon Wilt and Gehrman would pass me, so I moved quickly into the lead before the bell. As I accelerated, I felt that my moment of liberation had come. After being imprisoned for so many months in a world of stop-watches, my running suddenly became timeless, more than a machine in running shoes. I was transformed by the pure joy of making a physical effort for which my body was well prepared. The last lap of 56.7 sec. was the fastest time to date in a mile race, and I won in a new record time for this event, of 4 min. 8.3 sec.

My immediate reaction after the race was one of relief. I was delighted that I had after all succeeded. Though I had barely dared to admit it, I knew that in England the publicity about the race had been enormous, and the result had great/significance for the British public. On this occasion, rightly or wrongly, I had become a symbol in athletics of British sport against American, and for the sake of national prestige I felt I had to win. This was the third of a series of British victories, beginning with the Cambridge crew beating Harvard, followed by Randolph Turpin defeating Sugar Ray Robinson.

My 4 min. 9.9 sec. mile in New Zealand at Christmas 1950 had brought me to 40th place in the "all-time mile list." My Benjamin Franklin mile raised me to 20th place. I had still a long way to go, but I knew from my fast finish that I was now capable of a time near 4 min. 5 sec. Some of the American sports reporters complained that I made a mockery of the race by exploding in this unseemly fashion in the last lap, leaving Wilt 20 yards behind. One said, "Just keep him in England, that's all. That guy's murder over here." But most of them, with great respect for England's middle distance running, as typified by Wooderson and Lovelock, regarded my race as a victory in the "classic English manner."

In England, Harold Abrahams wrote, "What he needs now is confidence in his own ability. Modesty—a characteristic of Wooderson—in Bannister amounts to an almost complete reluctance to acknowledge his greatness. He has the brains to plan and dominate the Olympic Final as Lovelock did in 1936. To beat the world—and I believe he can—he must cultivate a purposeful aggression." Having great respect for Harold Abraham's judgment, I hoped that I was beginning to show a little of the necessary aggression.

The possibility of the four–minute mile was again mooted. I was full of doubt, but it costs nothing to talk about such things.

After doing some work in the University of Pennsylvania medical laboratories I returned to England. Public interest was even greater than I had imagined, and I was greeted with the headline, "No-circus victor returns home alone—just the way he runs."

141

Two weeks after my American race, on 12th May 1951 at the White City, I ran a mile in the same style, at the British Games. My opponents included Harting of the Netherlands and Browning Ross of U.S.A., winner of the Pan-American Games 1,500 metres title. I lay with the field at Harting's shoulder until 300 yards from the finish. Then Otenhajmer of Jugoslavia—a European Games 1,500 metres finalist—came up to my shoulder. This warning was enough—I was off. For the first time I heard the deep-throated White City roar as I made my finishing effort. It seems to give you new life, like a whiff of oxygen, so that you can leave the field standing, flying away like a wild duck startled from a clump of rushes. My time was 4 min. 9.2 sec., with a last lap of 56.9 sec., and I won by 30 yards.

This way of running may seem over-dramatic, but I wanted to ingrain in my mind the mental reactions required to train my body to respond with a fast finish. I aimed at producing a finishing top gear which I could sustain and which no one else could "live with." I could see that this kind of finish would be needed, as the standard of athletics was rising at successive international meetings. I thought of the closeness of the finishes in the middle distance races in the previous Olympic and European Games, and the bad luck that was apt to come to the "favourite."

I knew that no athlete would be safe unless he could strike just as Lovelock used to do and, however tired he felt, could maintain his ruthless speed to the finish.

142

This race had a sequel. Otenhajmer, having seen my finish at close hand, returned to Jugoslavia bent on revenge, as I found to my cost later.

Meanwhile in Britain public enthusiasm for athletics was growing. McDonald Bailey, had his usual victory in the 220 yards international race at these same British Games. On Whit Monday, Chris Chataway ran away with the international two-miles race in 9 min. 3.8 sec., winning by 30 yards, as one report said, "with devastating acceleration from the favourite Bannister spot—300 yards from home." I think the foreign competitors must have realised that the track was ours.

In the Middlesex Championships at Staines on 2nd June 1951, Arthur Wint beat me over 440 yards, with a new county record of 49.9 sec. I was not disgraced in this experiment over a shorter distance. It was a sodden grass track and my time was 51 sec.

Two weeks later Chris Chataway, running for Walton Athletic Club, challenged me at Chiswick in the Kinnaird Mile. Though I had great respect for Chataway's strength, I was prepared to gamble on my superior speed over the last 80 yards. I won by 5 yards in the slow overall time of 4 min. 16.2 sec. Chris Chataway came third, with Gordon Pirie in second place, already at 19 showing promise of becoming one of Britain's best distance runners.

I was criticised in some quarters for not taking the lead from the start, and for allowing myself to be "pushed around" in a race which I ought to have known I could win. I maintained that the important thing was to win, and that the time was a secondary consideration. On the same day, Jim Peters, who had made a come-back after his retirement in 1949, and had started his strenuous training programme, won his first Marathon race in 2 hr. 29 min. 24 sec., the fastest ever recorded by a British runner.

For the next Olympic Games the Scandinavian runners still seemed likely to provide the greatest threat in middle distance running. Boysen of Norway had great natural ability, and as he seemed incapable of staying behind, he might well become the Olympic 1,500 metres pace-maker.

So I accepted an invitation to run in Oslo. I hoped that I might also meet Lennart Strand who had equalled the world record for 1,500 metres. He was known as the "hare," through having set the pace in some of Gunder Haegg's record breaking runs. He was, however, such a nervous athlete that he frequently failed to produce his best form in big races.

When I arrived in Oslo the expected foreign opposition had melted away, and I was able to win a 1,500 metres race in the slow time of 3 min. 59 sec., equivalent to 4 min. 16 sec. for a mile. When I started sprinting 300 yards from the tape the crowd laughed at the obvious absence of competition, and their amusement only turned to applause over the last 20 yards.

144

A week later, on 26th June 1951, I made another visit to the Clonliffe Sports in Dublin, and raced on the grass track of Trinity College against Victor Milligan, a young Irish runner of great promise. It was another handicap race, and I started from scratch. I threaded my way through a field of eight, and needed a last lap of 57 sec. to shake off a very persistent challenge from Milligan.

On the following Saturday, 29th June 1951, there was a meeting at Southgate between Southgate Harriers and a team from Stockholm. I ran a ½ mile in 1 min. 53.6 sec., as a visitor, without scoring in the match.

On 5th July, only a week before the A.A.A. Championships, I flew to Finland; the opportunity of running on the new Olympic track at Helsinki was too good to miss. I wanted to be prepared for all eventualities. Before the race, Nurmi, the world's greatest distance runner in his time and still very well preserved, took away my split running shoes and arranged to have them stitched.

Taipale, Finland's best middle distance runner, was my chief rival in the 1,500 metres race. Because of the low evening sun his shadow on the back straight stretched out in front of me, and I could judge exactly the moment when he fell behind. It was a rain-soaked track, and my time was 3 min. 52.4 sec., equivalent to 4 min. 10 sec. for a mile.

Next came the big test of 1951, the British A.A.A.

Championships. My American race had given me a great reputation abroad, but an uneasy doubt of my ability lurked in the minds of many at home because I had not raced against my British rivals.

There were six British runners who had beaten 4 min. 15 sec. in 1951. Bill Nankeville, for whom I had the greatest respect, had already won the British Mile championship in the three preceding years. When we were together in Oslo he had told me that he was in good form and ready for anything. John Parlett, European 800 metres champion, had turned to miling. He had beaten Chataway in Oxford in a 4 min. 12 sec. mile, and had recently run a 4 min. 9.2 sec. mile in Paris to bear El Mabrouk. The A.A.A. field would also include the Northern runners Len Eyre and Alan Parker. It would be my first meeting with Parlett in an important mile, and I had not previously met Nankeville and Eyre at this distance.

I was called "the champion without a title," because I had still not won the British Mile Championship, which had become one of the toughest of national titles. Yet because of my racing abroad I had more prestige as a runner, and stood to lose more than the other competitors if I did not win. I was worried, lest I had done too much racing and travelling. During the season I had competed in nine major races and travelled thousands of miles.

In my mind the A.A.A. Mile became a test race for

146

the Olympic final. I knew I was not at my best. If, slightly jaded, I was not good enough to win I should not feel hopeful about the Olympic Final a year later. This was to be my last serious race before the Olympics. If I won, I decided I would temporarily stop racing in order to carry out my Olympic training programme.

By now there was no question of any "peak" being left in me. The season had been a symphony of diminuendos and crescendos. Now I was called on to stake everything in a race that was being dubbed "Britain's Mile of the Century." Might it not turn into a farce— "the smile of the century"—because no one would lead? I thought of the A.A.A. Mile Final in 1934, when Wooderson, Lovelock and Cornes were so busy watching each other that the time degenerated to a feeble 4 min. 26.6 sec. I hoped that the race would not become a mere battle of tactics.

The strain of the race itself was enormous. I felt more alone at the White City than when I had been 3,000 miles away in America. At first there was a great deal of timidity in front and pushing from behind, as though we were all chasing a will-o'-the-wisp. Then Parker took the lead. As he did not have a fast finish over this distance his only hope was to speed up the pace from the start. There was a moment of exquisite anxiety just after the bell, pleasurable because I now had the sense of command.

Parker was still leading and I could distinctly feel

147

Parlett hesitating at my shoulder. For a moment I was wedged between them and nearly boxed in. I took the lead decisively, slipping between them and brushing their shoulders as I did so. This was evidently the correct moment to seize the initiative. I had to make the first move, but have sufficient strength to resist the late challenge I expected from Parlett.

I rested for a moment round the next to last bend, knowing that I could not sustain a sprint for the full 440 yards. Just before the back straight I had enough reserves left for a weaker burst, which I maintained to the finish. I had never been so exhausted before as I crossed the line. The time was 4 min. 7.8 sec., my fastest, and a best championship performance, but my last lap of 59.1 sec. was slow for me and lacked fire. In no circumstances could my performance be described as rapturous running. I was racing to the limit of my strength, and my main feeling was relief that I had won.

This was my best season, and after eight successful mile and 1,500 metres races I decided I had run enough. But there were still obligations. In the triangular match at Dunoon on 28th July 1951, I ran a half-mile for England. I decided beforehand that 1 min. 58 sec. would beat Scotland and Ireland, and I was determined to run no faster. Frank Evans, also running for England, won in 1 min. 57.3 sec. I was in second place about six yards behind, and the heavens descended on me for this ignominious defeat!

148

On August Bank Holiday I ran my third and most light-hearted race against Arthur Wint in a Britain-France match at the White City. We were comfortably ahead of the French half-milers, and at 660 yards I very nearly seized the lead from Wint. But he fought me off to the last bend, and when I attacked again in the finishing straight it was too late. Wint's time was 1 min. 52.1 sec., mine 1 min. 52.9 sec. I had the satisfaction that for once in my life I might have given the great man an anxious moment!

Each season now, sooner or later, the moment came when I almost hated athletics, because of the publicity attached to my track appearances. Somehow I felt this almost prostituted my running. It left me no freedom or joy to run as I pleased. So in August of 1951 I lost myself in Scotland for two weeks, walking, climbing, and sleeping in the open.

One day I had been swimming, and to get warm I started running. Soon I was running across the moor to a distant part of the coast of Kintyre. It was near evening and fiery sun clouds were chasing over to Arran. It began to rain, and the sun shining brightly behind me cast a rainbow ahead. It gave me the feeling that I was cradled in the rainbow arc as I ran.

I felt I was running back to all the primitive joy that my season had destroyed. At the coast the rainbow was lost in the myriad particles of spray, beaten up by the breakers as they crashed vainly against the granite rocks. I grew calmer as I sat watching pebbles lazily rolling to

149

and fro where the fury had gone from the waves. I turned back.

The gulls were crying overhead and a herd of wild goats was silhouetted against the headland. I started to run again with the sun in my eyes nearly blinding me. I could barely distinguish slippery rock from heathery turf or bog, yet my feet did not slip or grow weary now —they had new life and confidence. I ran in a frenzy of speed, drawn on by an unseen force. The sun sank, setting the forest ablaze, and turning the sky to dull smoke. Then tiredness came on and my bleeding feet tripped me. I rolled down a heather topped bank and lay there happily exhausted.

I came back from Scotland thoroughly refreshed, but I was not ready for running spikes. I had done no regular training since the A.A.A. Mile, five weeks earlier. But I had to run in Belgrade, and with resignation I packed my bags once more and flew out with the British team. To my knowledge no Jugoslav had ever broken the equivalent of a 4 min. 10 sec. mile, so I was hopeful. In this 1,500 metres race, on 25th August 1951, a Jugoslav wearing a red vest shot into the lead at the gun. Could this be Otenhajmer, whom I had beaten earlier in the year at the White City in London?

For a moment I felt reassured. It must be a pacemaker, certain to drop out at any minute. But as the lap times were announced, first lap 59 sec., half mile 2 min. 1.6 sec., I realised the pace was too fast for me. I had never run the first half-mile in less than 2 min. 6 sec.

150

I was ten yards back waiting for Otenhajmer to crack—
but it was I who cracked. At 2½ laps it was clear that
Otenhajmer, out of revenge, had risen superbly to the
occasion, in his own stadium before his own countrymen.

Painfully I strove to close the gap. At the bell I managed to reach him, but the effort was too great and I was
unable to hold him. His neat crisp stride never tired. I
was beginning to fade on the back straight. My legs
seemed like heavy timbers, my chest stretched to burst-
ing point. I do not know how I reached the tape.

Otenhajmer had run a wonderful race, and finished
amid a tornado of applause in 3 min. 47 sec., the fastest
time of the year, and the equivalent of a 4 min. 5.5 sec.
mile. My time was 3 min. 48.6 sec., a new record for
me, though I was completely out of training. It was
twelve hours before the pain in my legs passed off.

Two days later I caught dysentery and was unfit to
run in Athens. When I attempted in Turkey to run a
half mile race, I was so ill that I turned a bluish colour
and finished last. It was my most disappointing tour.

I had grown slack after my peak in the A.A.A. Championships, and this overwhelming defeat in Jugoslavia
was what I needed to put me in the right frame of mind
for the Olympic Games. At Helsinki any runner might
excel himself exactly as Otenhajmer had done. I could
not afford to take things easily during the winter.

Another surprise came at the end of the season to

disturb my dreams. Landqvist of Sweden, who beat me after my return from America in 1949, ran a 1,500 metres race in 3 min. 44.8 sec. with Olla Alberg 0.7 sec. behind. These times were the equivalent of a 4 min. 3 sec. mile —four seconds faster than I had ever done!

# CHAPTER ELEVEN

# PREPARATION FOR OLYMPIC GAMES
## HELSINKI 1952

*"Now! now,"* cried the Queen, *"Faster, faster!"*
THROUGH THE LOOKING GLASS.

In the winter of 1951-52 I started on my Olympic plan. Because of the tremendous nervous strain I suffered during races, I believed that excessive competition was essentially harmful to someone of my temperament. So I did not run in any cross-country races during the winter. I decided not to start running on the track until February, and did most of my training near my home round the grass cricket field of Harrow School.

This was nearly a mile round, enlivened by its slope and by the variety of elms and poplars that surrounded it. I did not have time to train until evening, when it was dark. Often I was tired from standing in hospital wards, operating theatres or tube trains. It needed an enormous effort to make myself change into my running kit, but once I had taken the plunge the run always refreshed and invigorated me. I never ran for longer than half an hour, never timed myself with a stop watch.

Running in the dark has always had a strange fascination for me. Being unable to see the expanse of ground very far ahead I am not depressed by the distance yet to be covered, and have a sense of going at great speed. The velvety ensheathing blackness makes me feel at one with the world, as if the earth were moving with me. This gives great power to my running.

There was some risk, because the field had no lights. One evening I was leaping across a stream in one corner of the field instead of crossing over a tiny bridge. I slipped and fell, and the sharp concrete edge cut deeply into my shin bone and the flesh. In the dark I could not see how deep the cut was, and I tried to continue running. The blood was flowing freely, so I came home and went to the hospital. They cut away the dirt and stitched the wound, but it was a month before I could run again.

At Christmas the American ranking for the Olympics appeared in the Press. I was given fourth place! Willi Slijkhuis of Holland, the reigning European champion, was selected as the winner, Landqvist of Sweden as second, with the equivalent of a 4 min. 3 sec. mile to his credit, and Otenhajmer of Jugoslavia third.

There was one occasion when I ran myself to exhaustion. I had spent the afternoon watching Oxford's victory over Cambridge in the boat race. I felt frustrated that I had not been able to take part in their magnificent struggle of utter exhaustion from rowing in company and in time with the rest of the crew.

I went out running as soon as I reached home. The snow was falling and already lay about four inches deep.

154

No one had crossed it, and every step I took left its impression behind on the virgin whiteness. I ran and ran until I was exhausted.

In the spring of 1952 the furore over my training methods was let loose and continued all summer. One writer said, "Bannister needs serious tests," and another, "Is it fair to take Bannister's record as good enough?" Some light relief was provided by a third writer, who under a headline, "Bannister won't turn a hair," reported that I was "likely to be paced by an electric hare at the White City," as part of my training for the Olympic Games! An appearance of truth was given to this rumour by a newspaper photograph, obviously faked, showing me panting behind an electric hare.

I was building myself up for one supreme explosive effort on 26th July 1952 in the Olympic Final at Helsinki. I had intended that the A.A.A. Championships of 1951 should be my last fiercely competitive mile until Helsinki. I decided that I would not defend my A.A.A. Mile title in the summer of 1952, but would run in the half-mile instead. This would take away none of my freshness or strength, and would give me sharper tactical experience. There was much surprised comment, but I did not allow it to disturb me.

I did not expect people to understand my scheme of training. I only hoped that they would be patient with me and trust that I was doing my best to prepare for the Olympic race. But everyone seemed to know better than I how I should train. I had no coach or adviser,

155

and hence no alibi if things went wrong. I had to carry the full weight of decisions myself. I now regretted that by running so fast the previous year I had added fuel to the fire.

Everyone wants to give good advice to the favourite, and if there is a mishap, they enjoy the feeling that it comes as the result of not following their advice. I knew I must store enough nervous energy to explode at the right moment. I could not afford to squander preciously hoarded nervous and physical reserves beforehand in unnecessary gladiatorial combats. An Olympic victory is an honour that may come only once to a nation; for me to achieve it, I must have an absolutely single aim.

By May 1952, five runners had already bettered the existing Olympic record. It is foolhardy to predict the winner in such a field. To come even last in the Final should really be regarded as a great honour, but I knew that if I were beaten by inches or feet in one of sport's most exacting events, I should be called a failure.

In my first race of the season on 28th May at Motspur Park, I placated my critics for a time by running a 1 min. 53 sec. half-mile for London University against Oxford, with a good first lap of 54.4 sec. More interest attached to the Inter-Hospitals Mile at Motspur Park on Saturday, 7th June, when I was described as "coming out of splendid isolation." I had to set my own pace from the start, and won a "solo" mile in 4 min. 10.6 sec. against a head wind. I felt a mile at this speed should have come more easily, but perhaps I was hoping for too

156

much. In the corresponding meeting in 1936, Lovelock came third in 4 min. 28 sec.—he did not believe in getting fit too soon! I was very satisfied with my time trials at this time—¾-mile in 3 min. 1.6 sec., and 660 yards in 80.2 sec., which is the equivalent of a 1 min. 50 sec. half-mile.

As the Olympics grew closer my critics became more clamorous, mainly over my decision not to run a mile against first class opposition in the A.A.A. Championships. After this match the Olympic team was to be selected. To run or not to run, that was the question.

The main charges levelled against me were:

*First:*
Bannister is almost assuming that the selectors have already picked him—"expecting to be chosen virtually on trust." Is this fair to the selectors or right for Bannister? Is there one law for the established athlete and another for the lesser athlete?

My answer to this, if I had been asked for it, would have been that Olympic selection in Britain is based, not on one race, but on the total impression of ability judged by recent performances. In other countries, America for example, there are rules as strict as the laws of the Medes and Persians. The team is selected on the result of one race only. Dillard, the world record holder for the high hurdles, was excluded from that event in the 1948 Olympics simply because he had an off day at the trial. He qualified for the sprint, however, and showed his sense

**157**

of frustration, and possibly contempt, at this treatment, by winning the 100 metres Olympic Final at Wembley. Rules are meant to be broken sometimes!

America has not won an Olympic 1,500 metres title since 1908. This may be due as much to their training methods as to a system of selection demanding that an athlete should give his best a month before the Olympic Games. I could appreciate the advantage Lovelock had as the representative of a small country, not insisting on severe races as a qualification for selection.

*Second:*

By "refusing to do any competitive miling this season," and refusing to defend my National Mile title, I was avoiding my most serious rivals.

My answer to this would have been that because of my way of training and running, a race with the nervous strain of the A.A.A. Mile Final would prejudice my performance in the Olympic Games. I did not want to throw away an Olympic title for a lesser crown. I respected my rivals in Britain, but I had beaten them all the previous summer, and did not consider them as serious challengers at Helsinki. The Olympic standard was quite different, and I saw no useful purpose in exhausting myself needlessly.

*Third:*

This was the most serious charge—that by limiting my public appearances, and "training in secret," I was harming the sport and giving nothing to it. Our athletes were, after all, dependent on the generosity of the public to enable their Olympic expenses to be met.

Problems of duty are always most difficult. Even an amateur athlete, who runs simply because he enjoys it, has a duty towards the public. After much consideration I decided that it was my duty to train as I thought best for the Olympic Final, whatever that might involve. It was a goal so high as to be worth every sacrifice. No compromise was possible. I tried to be influenced as little as possible by the doubts and anxieties of others— once the decision was taken. If others thought my methods madness, then I must go on alone.

*Fourth:*
"Refusing to put himself in the charge of a Grade A coach." I have discussed my feelings about coaching elsewhere in this book.

So I went on alone, but I knew that in the bitterness and criticism that had been aroused I had exchanged the sympathy of the public for a begrudging permission to go my own way in training. This seemed implicit in the final plea—"leave Bannister alone."

Only by success would my lone furrow be justified. Why did my freedom of decision always seem so hard to win? I was now cornered. Victory at Helsinki was the only way out. Perhaps I strove to create this situation, so that in desperation I would be forced to get the

159

last ounce out of myself. It was probable that the 1952 Olympic Games would be my only Olympics. Running was not my only interest, and I could not afford to spend another four years, jeopardising my medical future, with this exciting distraction. I was glad in a way that the chance could only come once. Success or failure at one throw, this seemed right.

The Queen and Princess Margaret came to see the A.A.A. Championships on 21st June 1952. Nankeville won the mile race in 4 min. 9.8 sec. from John Landy, and I won the half-mile in 1 min. 51.5 sec. with Albert Webster second. Wasn't it more usual for me to run in the mile, the Queen asked, as she handed me the cup.

In running this half-mile I drew off very little of my carefully husbanded reserves of energy, though it was the second fastest half-mile ever run in these Championships. I hoped this would silence the critics, but the damage was already done.

A week or so later, on 5th July at the Triangular Match at the White City, there was more fluttering in the dovecotes. Albert Webster turned the tables on me by beating me by a yard in a slowish half-mile of 1 min. 55.7 sec. It was only three weeks before the Olympics, and I was saving myself. I ran as hard as I could, but half my mind was saying, "wait for the day that matters," and Webster outsprinted me. I appreciated then the strength and promise which he proved later in the Games at Helsinki.

The Press had two ideas about this defeat. Mostly

160

they said it was the result of my self-imposed lack of racing experience, and maintained this was a mistake. A more subtle comment was that I had planned this defeat to escape from the limelight I never sought or wanted.

Almost the same day, Werner Lueg of Germany stole some of this limelight by equalling the world record of 3 min. 43 sec. for 1,500 metres in the German championships. Dohrow was second in 3 min. 44.8 sec., also well inside the existing Olympic record.

But my own training was going well. Ten days before the Helsinki Final I ran my last time trial at Motspur Park. Chataway led for the first lap and a half, and I completed a ¾-mile in 2 min. 52.9 sec. The time was unbelievable, with each lap faster than the previous one —58.5, 57.5 and 56.9 sec. I had never run at such speed before, and I rank this as equal to if not better than a 4-minute mile. I felt joyously full of the running that I had restrained for so long.

Though this trial did not take much out of me, it was nearly four whole seconds better than the unofficial world record of 2 min. 56.6 sec., set up by Arne Andersson of Sweden in 1945, and my own English native record of 2 min. 56.8 sec., at Motspur Park on 17th April, 1951. I knew that my best distance was ¾-mile, but I never imagined I could run as fast as this.

The Olympic distance of 1,500 metres, which suits me better than a mile, is only 320 yards longer than ¾-mile. I felt now that in a Final race, with a day's rest after the

161

heat, I could beat even the world record. This should be fast enough to win at Helsinki. I bound those who had seen the trial to secrecy, because it was only valuable as a boost for my own state of mind. I felt very happy.

Next morning I opened my paper and saw the headlines, "Semi-finals for the Olympic 1,500 metres." There were to be races on three consecutive days, heats, semi-finals and then the Final. I could hardly believe it. In just the length of time it took to read those few words the bottom had fallen out of my hopes. There had never been semi-finals before.

It was crazy for such an exhausting distance. No man who trained as I did could possibly run three good races in three consecutive days. There must be a mistake. There would be protests. Everyone would surely realise how absurd it was.

Whatever the number of competitors it was unnecessary to hold semi-finals. All that was needed was severer heats—with as few as two in each heat qualifying for the Final. Just when I had become certain that my training method was right, this change in the Olympic programme made nonsense of it, and denied me all chance of vindicating my ideas. I felt the victim of circumstance, because I knew the change would hit me harder than the other competitors, most of whom had been training for an hour or so daily, with very severe interval running. With three races their tougher training gave them an advantage; my scheme of training was

162

suited to two races, with an interval between to give the necessary edge of freshness.

My personal disappointment was, after all, only a ripple in the Olympic whirlpool, but I could not help feeling the victim of fate. I would have no chance of proving my theory, because the racing conditions had been changed overnight. This was the frame of mind in which I travelled to Helsinki with Chataway, after the main party, and five days before my first heat.

# CHAPTER TWELVE

# OLYMPIC GAMES

## HELSINKI 1952

*"For some of us are out of breath."*
THROUGH THE LOOKING GLASS.

In HELSINKI the Games differed from those at Wembley because of the uneasiness over Russia's entry. This was the first time she had sent a full team to an international meeting—her team in the 1950 European Games was not at full strength.

The modern Olympic Games succeed in bringing the countries together in a way which must be the envy of every well-meaning politician. It reminds one of the fact that during the ancient Olympic Games a truce was declared, and the contestants were granted safe passage through enemy territory.

I am convinced that rivalry in the Olympic Games does not aggravate existing relations between the nations. Quarrels and appeals—which are often greatly magnified in the Press—are usually the result of the tension created by the races themselves and not due to any international ill-feeling. Such quarrels might and do take place at any

164

sports meeting where no international aspect is involved.

Somehow we must guard against the Games becoming a struggle between nations, instead of sporting encounters between individuals of representative teams who have a common interest in sport for its own sake.

One evening it was arranged that a group of British athletes and officials should visit the Russian camp. We travelled by bus from the Olympic village at Helsinki where all the teams except the Russian and satellite teams were staying. The Russians had taken over a school some 20 miles from Helsinki in the direction of the ice-free port of Porkkala, which Finland had leased to the Russians as a naval base after the war. The Russians were reputed to have big guns in Porkkala trained on Helsinki.

We dismounted from the bus in front of the Russian camp, a large technical school set in pine forests. We stood waiting under a gigantic portrait of Stalin stretched over the front of the building. The words C.C.P.R.— the Russian equivalent for U.S.S.R.—were printed in foot high letters above. Stalin, in a plain suit with a raincoat slung over his arm, was smiling benignly upon us from the poster. There was a depressing background to the portrait, arid desert punctuated by oil derricks and electricity pylons, which stood out like bristles on a porcupine's back. Beneath the portrait were three smaller pictures of the Presidents of Roumania, Hungary and Czechoslovakia.

We felt embarrassed and slightly apprehensive. We

165

began to wonder if anyone was going to meet us. Gradually Russian interpreters became entangled in the perimeter of our group as if by accident, and began speaking to the less prominent among us, apparently ignoring the officials in charge. But it is so easy to misjudge the situation—perhaps we had not arrived at the time expected.

Gradually we were made welcome. After much handshaking the chief of their delegation, who looked like a former heavy-weight wrestler, met Mr. Philip Noel-Baker, the Commandant of the British team.

Mr. Philip Noel-Baker himself competed in the 1,500 metres at the Olympic Games in 1912 and 1920, when he assisted in British victories. Ever since he has kept up his love of athletics. Perhaps because of his own middle distance running, he has shown special interest in my track efforts, and has always been one of my closest advisers.

One of the Russians was asking for me—which seemed very strange as I had only decided to make the visit an hour or so previously. The whole evening had a bewildering alternation of planning and confusion—of friendliness and distrust. The leader of their delegation was the assistant director of Soviet sport, who had come to England in 1945 with the Dynamos football team from Moscow, and more recently with the Russian chess team. "Let us watch our little ceremony," my interpreter friend said. We walked through the camp until at the entrance to the dining room we were shown a large board, like a school honours board. "Here we honour

166

our victors each day and inscribe their names in gold, silver or bronze." The list included winners from satellite countries. We stood trying to recognise the names in Russian lettering.

"We have no gold medals," I said, turning to my interpreter.

"But you are a small country," he replied, not very tactfully, and smiled at his little joke.

There seemed to be some hitch in the ceremony itself, so we crossed the room and sat down at long tables in the centre, my interpreter beside me. Anufryev, the Russian 5,000 metres champion, sat opposite me. The Russians did not avail themselves of the services of the charming Finnish girls who waited on us in the main Olympic village. They brought their own waiters from Russia, who suddenly rushed in. I was hoping for caviare and Russian steaks. Instead they offered us fancy cakes from dishes already on the table.

The interpreter told me he had been sent out from Moscow. He did all kinds of public relations work. Though he had little knowledge of sport he seemed prepared to answer my questions freely about his life and his country. I felt he was being frank and that we were establishing a genuine understanding.

The waiters descended upon us again—this time with oranges—perhaps they had not expected us for dinner after all. I was getting very hungry, and the fierce spirits offered to us were difficult to swallow without food.

Then the speeches began. The Russian director would

167

speak a sentence and the Russians would applaud vigorously. This was interpreted, and we ourselves would applaud, not quite so vigorously. Finally the speaker himself added a round of applause of his own. When his self-adulation was over he launched on his next sentence, and the process was repeated. In this comic atmosphere it was difficult to believe in the sincerity of the Russians, or indeed the sincerity with which we welcomed their gesture of friendship.

"We admire your team," he said, "and earnestly request your brotherhood in sport, friendship and peace. Though there are clouds overhead the stars shine brightly . . ." I felt a great sympathy for those who have to sit through United Nations and similar proceedings.

Before we left, the interpreter seemed suddenly worried and turned to me, "What do you think the Americans will do if we win more medals than they do?"

"Why, nothing," I replied, "except to try even harder next time."

The 1,500 metres struggle opened on Thursday 24th July with six heats, the first four in each heat qualifying for the semi-finals on the following day. In my heat my opponents included my rival Otenhajmer of Jugoslavia, El Mabrouk of France, Landy of Australia, McMillen of U.S.A., and Marshall of New Zealand.

We had a scrambling race. No one wanted to lead and so there was a very speedy last lap. El Mabrouk won in 3 min. 55.8 sec., the equivalent of a 4 min. 13 sec. mile, and I came third in 3 min. 56 sec. This did

168

not exhaust me unduly, but I had not been sleeping much all week and I got no sleep afterwards. I was sharing a room with my Oxford friends; Chris Chataway was in the next bed, then Nick Stacey, who kept telling us among other things that he was "the fastest white man in Europe," and finally Alan Dick, the quarter miler. Ours must have been the untidiest room in the Olympic village, strewn with open suit-cases, empty milk bottles, and half opened packets of patent medicines for every imagined ailment. We spent most of the day just lying on our unmade beds, reading books and talking. It was not that we lacked the energy to make our beds or tidy the room. We simply existed in a state of complete suspension, in which nothing seemed important until our races were over. We were thinking all the time about the precious fractions of seconds that would make us champions or failures.

With our divided minds we could talk lightly, read escapist books, or even discuss serious subjects. Then quite suddenly the facade would break down and the underlying current of our thoughts would surge upwards. We would admit our intolerable anxiety, talk of our chances for a moment, and swear that when the Olympics were over we would never set foot on a running track again.

Having relieved the tension a little we would go on hiding our feelings for another interval. We rose from our beds carefully, fearing we might pull a muscle—the

169

last disgrace. At night we crawled wearily back, not expecting to sleep.

It was well that there were moments of light relief, which usually came from Nick Stacey. Once he stood up saying, "I'd better rehearse that victory ceremony, just in case . . ." The rest of us burst out laughing—our chances seemed so hopeless. He stood at the end of his bed, on a piece of Finnish box-like furniture that was a fair replica of the winner's rostrum in the Olympic stadium. Alan and Chris pretended to have come second and third, and stood on either side of him. He bowed his head as he received the imaginary gold medal, murmuring modestly, "I'm so glad, sir—for my country." I was just beginning an imitation of the victory fanfare when the illusion broke down, and we collapsed laughing on our beds.

"What makes a man superhuman?" asked Chris, thinking of his rival Zatopek. "He's the only great runner in the whole bunch at Helsinki. The rest—why they're just hacks." This was Chris's favourite word for runners who would train for hours on end, and yet could not make a good sprint at the finish. Chris could not run for long without getting bored by it. Running for him as—for all of us—was a sport, not a business, and he assumed that those who could run for hours must be completely insensitive.

It did not seem to matter what training they did provided they ran for longer than anyone else. Such runners could plough through fields or round running tracks wearing army boots or running shoes until their minds quietly died. They could drive their senseless coach-driven bodies to within an inch of the grave. Perhaps we were cast in a different mould, we decided—hastily putting together the last pieces of the jig-saw puzzle in our minds, and, because it flattered us, dashing off without seeing whether the pieces fitted.

"How can Zatopek do it?" I asked. "He has the prospect of three gold medals in a week, and a fourth for his wife, who may win the javelin event."

"Zatopek isn't human in his achievement," Chris said, "yet he's as intelligent as any other athlete running. Here we are doing a third of the running Zatopek's doing this week. While he goes for a 20-mile training run on his only free day, we lie here panting with exhaustion, moaning that the gods are unkind to us, and that we're too intelligent to train hard. It's all nonsense."

"Did you hear about Zatopek and the Australian reporter?" I said. "The night before the 10,000 metres he burst into Zatopek's room at midnight. We should have thrown him out angrily, and blamed our failure the following day on his disturbing our non-existent sleep. But Zatopek gave him a 20-minute interview. Then when he found the reporter hadn't a bed for the night he offered him half his own."

"This is a stupid book," cried Alan, "in fact it's the silliest book I have ever read—a hundred pages and nothing's happened. In the last week I've started seven books all chosen by experts for their excitement and

171

suspense, and I haven't been able to finish one of them. As soon as I get home I'm going to take up writing!"

There was a knock on the door and a team mate sauntered in. He did not want anything except the comfort and relief that no one could give him. In a wretched climax of self-centredness he was attempting to lose himself for a moment—as it was very easy for him to do in the untidiness of our room. We developed a reputation for being insane humorists. Our room became a sanctuary sought by those confined in rooms where the tension was even greater.

Chris Chataway's ordeal in the 5,000 metres Final gave me some idea of what to expect. At the beginning of the last lap Chataway, Zatopek, Mimoun (France) and Schade (Germany) were all together. Chris tried to run clear of them in the back straight, and his magnificent effort carried him to the front. But his burst had come too soon and he could not maintain it to the tape. I called out, almost yelled to Chris to keep going, but could feel within me that his strength was fading and his legs wavering.

The three giants passed him. They seemed at that moment almost unreasonably bigger, older and stronger than Chataway. Chris stumbled and collapsed on the last bend. He recovered courageously and finished fifth, 60 yards behind the first three runners. I felt sick and hollow with sympathy for him.

It made me appreciate how fatal it could be to make my finishing effort too soon in a field of this standard.

How was one to judge the appropriate moment amid the clamour of the crowd, and in the heat and fear of the race? It seemed unfair that so much should depend on the decision of a moment, but this was inherent in the race. The finalists in the 1,500 metres would have no second innings in which to redeem a failure.

In the semi-finals on Friday there were two groups of twelve runners, with the first six in each race to qualify for the Final. It seemed almost ludicrous for the best milers in the world, divided into two semi-finals, to be racing against each other the day before the Final. But this was just what happened. The coveted places were left in dispute until the last stride.

In my semi-final Jose Barthel romped home first in 3 min. 50.4 sec., equivalent to a 4 min. 8 sec. mile. The last lap was under 60 sec. Barthel was known to belong to the toughest training school and looked very fresh afterwards. I finished fifth, blown and unhappy. Only two-fifths of a second separated the qualifiers. Johansson of Finland won the other semi-final in the faster time of 3 min. 49.4 sec., but there was a gap of 1.6 sec. between the qualifiers.

The following night was one of the most unpleasant I have ever spent. My legs ached and I was unable to sleep. I felt I hated running. For the last few months I had tried to go on with my hospital work for as long as possible, to lose myself and forget the thoughts that preyed on my mind. Now with the whole athletic world

173

concentrated in a few square miles all sense of perspective was lost. Around me every man was giving his best —fighting to the last gasp.

I thought of the stadium to be filled next day with 70,000 people, all waiting and watching. I thought too of the moment when victory was in the balance and when I must galvanise my tired limbs to fresh effort. However slowly the seconds and minutes passed the moment for the race must come, sometime, somehow. The agony of suspense could not last for ever.

In my sleepless nights I had run the race a thousand times. Sometimes I won, my pulse racing, my temples pounding, sleep further and further off. Sometimes I lost, and I lay there in a cold sweat until my mind brought me to the starting post again with another chance of winning.

So we lay there, four of us, tied in knots with anxiety. We all knew that the emotional satisfaction of those few moments of intense excitement, win or lose, had bitten deep into our personalities. We should all want to try again—however much we swore that nothing would drag us on the running track again. Our success on the track was only a very small part of our lives but we hoped it had taught us a discipline that was transferable to other spheres.

I still had a lot to learn about my own self-control. We all realised more about our weakness and strength as we wound up our minds for the trial. Each tackled in

174

his own way the problem of gaining the necessary self-control. It was strange to be hoarding every available atom of energy, simply to dissipate it all—more than we ever dreamt we possessed—on one extravagant outburst.

Saturday brought the Final—the third consecutive day of trial. Eyre had been eliminated in his heat, and Nankeville in the semi-final, so I was the only representative of Great Britain left. The finalists included two Germans, Lueg and Lamers, two Americans, McMillen and Dreutzler, two Swedes, Aberg and Eriksson, Johansson of Finland, El Mabrouk of France, Boysen of Norway, MacMillan of Australia, and Barthel of Luxembourg.

I hardly had the strength to warm up. As I walked out in front of those 70,000 spectators, my step had no spring, my face no colour. The ruthless fighting of the semi-final, the worry and lack of sleep, had exhausted me. There had been too little time between the races to regain my strength. As I stood at the start I felt a loyalty to all sports lovers waiting at home. Everyone wished me well but they could not help me here.

The world was expecting the supremacy of one of these twelve runners to be revealed by a stroke of genius. 'Ve stood there, twelve anxious men waiting for the start. Twelve is far too many for a 1,500 metres race of this class. We pushed and struggled along, continually changing position. I ran more sensibly than in the semi-final. I was content to keep to the inside—because I was

175

too tired to struggle. Lamers of Germany led for the first and second laps. Then Lueg, also of Germany, went into the lead. At the bell on the third lap we were five abreast waiting for someone to try to break away. Barthel came up alongside.

Only a minute more and it would be all over. On the back straight I forced myself to move up to Lueg's shoulder. I lay second before the last bend perfectly poised for my finishing effort.

This was the crucial moment, for which I had waited so long. But my legs were aching, and I had no strength left to force them faster. I had a sickening feeling of exhaustion and powerlessness as Barthel came past me, chased by McMillen (U.S.A.). They both caught and passed Lueg who was also slowing down. The race was won by inches in 3 min. 45.2 sec. by Barthel—the tough little athlete from a country with a population no greater than an English town.

I came fourth, and a few yards covered the first six. The first eight of us had broken the previous Olympic record (3 min. 47.8 sec. by J. E. Lovelock) in 1936. As I crossed the line I grabbed at Lueg to prevent myself from sprawling on the track. I had never known such exhaustion, but I was very happy that the ordeal was over. My friends told me afterwards they had expected me to be last in the Final because I looked so tired. By now I was resigned and philosophical. It had been a great race and I felt proud to have come fourth.

The final placings were:

| | | Min. | Sec. |
|---|---|---|---|
| 1. J. Barthel (Luxembourg) .. | .. | 3 | 45.2 |
| 2. R. McMillen (U.S.A.) .. | .. | 3 | 45.2 |
| 3. W. Lueg (West Germany) | .. | 3 | 45.4 |
| 4. R. G. Bannister (Great Britain) | .. | 3 | 46.0 |
| 5. P. El Mabrouk (France) .. | .. | 3 | 46.0 |
| 6. R. Lamers (West Germany) | .. | 3 | 46.8 |
| 7. O. Aberg (Sweden) | .. | 3 | 47.0 |
| 8. I. Eriksson (Sweden) | .. | 3 | 47.6 |
| 9. D. MacMillan (Australia) .. | .. | 3 | 49.6 |
| 10. D. Johansson (Finland) | .. | 3 | 49.8 |
| 11. A. Boysen (Norway) | .. | 3 | 51.4 |
| 12. W. Dreutzler (U.S.A.) .. | .. | 3 | 56.0 |

I also felt great admiration for Jose Barthel as he climbed the Olympic rostrum. He was a worthy victor, tougher as well as faster than the rest of us. I knew his happiness must be without limit. He was strong and courageous, and fortune had smiled on him. No one could begrudge him his success. As Barthel stood on the rostrum, hearing his country's anthem played for the first time in the Games, he raised his hand to wipe away a tear. His great strength was overcome by the tide of joy. Then he turned the movement into a wave of gratitude to the crowd.

Many things could have gone wrong before we even reached the Final. The ordeal was now over, and in the great joy of that single moment the agony of the previous week was quite forgotten. I had found new meaning in the Olympic words that the important thing was not the winning but the taking part—not the conquering but the fighting well. All week I had seen the interplay of success and failure, and felt no bitterness at the outcome of my own race. My only chance to win an Olympic title was over. I had seen some who had been beaten when with a luckier position they might have won. Others had won and I had been happy for them.

There was some criticism in the British Press over my failure. Britain had not won a gold medal on the track, and I was the last chance. Some writers were more considerate, and asked how coming fourth in a race of this kind, and breaking the Olympic record, could possibly be called failure. Other writers suggested that my four-year plan had failed because I had put the stopwatch before running in races. After a headline, "No—Roger wasn't nearly tough enough," one writer ended his criticism with, "I feel like suing British athletes for breach of promise."

A letter appeared in *The Times* of 13th August 1952, replying to criticism that the Press were unfair—"Staff writers were almost unanimous that the 1,500 metres Final showed this athlete's (Bannister's) training methods to be wrong; an error to which many of them had drawn attention earlier in the summer, only to find it condoned by British athletic officials to the point of Bannister's abstention from competitive running over the distance."

To me it was failure—when the immediate joy of relief had faded. But what use was there in revealing the speed

178

of my last time trial before the Games? I did not have second sight. How could I have foreseen the arbitrary revision of the programme at the last minute—a change which made nonsense at one stroke of a long year's training schedule—right or wrong. If one fails in the Olympics there is no second chance—the years of waiting would seem an eternity of hopelessness. Any attempt to explain away a disappointment is taken as an admission of failure.

The Games were a great success. Barthel's triumph in the 1,500 metres was to me symbolic of the Olympic spirit that seems to safeguard the Games from harmful influences. The attitude of every nation to sport is different—as distinctive as its own art or political system, because all are reflections of national temperament. But no nation can wreck the Olympic movement, when to run costs an athlete no more than food and shelter, a pair of spikes, and willingness to drive himself to the furthest limit of exhaustion.

After the Games there was a post-mortem on the corpse of British sport. Cure-alls are as popular in sport as they are in matters of health. Could we convince ourselves that we had not failed, that it was merely the astonishing ability of the others to beat us? We had seen for the first time a state of affairs, now common, in which record after record was broken by the winning athletes. Should we have to adopt the Russian or American systems to produce better athletes, or should we continue to be ourselves? To regard sport as a hobby is surely more of a virtue than a vice, and is much closer to the Greek ideal of the complete man than is the athletic machine. If we keep our own attitude other countries will respect us more and we shall still enjoy our sport.

The Helsinki Olympic Games were a turning point in my life, in more ways than one. Until then I had on the whole been successful in all the races that mattered to me. I do not find it easy to be over-confident, but an Olympic victory might easily have made me so. My opponents were stronger, physically and psychologically. I was not able to bear the responsibility thrust on my shoulders, the terrible burden of having to win. I had tried to bear it alone by developing an attitude of isolation without any buffers between myself and success or failure.

I realised how much luck there is in sport. No amount of planning and foresight by the athlete can safeguard against organisational changes. I had taken myself and my one goal too seriously. My gamble on one event had been too great—was it possible for me to justify the faith that others placed in me?

# CHAPTER THIRTEEN

# SO NEAR AND YET—

## *1953*

*"Why dost thou run so many mile about"*
RICHARD III.

EVERYONE has to give up something for the sake of his sport. To justify my sacrifices I had to have some goal. I was not prepared to travel round the country, running in athletic meetings here and there, never improving and with no new aim in view.

My hospital work was becoming more pressing, and I came near to stopping running after the Olympic Games. The European and Empire Games were not due to take place until 1954, in the year of my medical finals. There was no point in running for just one year in 1953 when there were no outstanding international events My choice was therefore between stopping running at once, and continuing for two more years to see what 1954 would bring. It was almost certain that full-time hospital work would prevent me from taking part in the Olympic Games of 1956.

I spent about two months turning the problem over in

my mind while I was doing routine work as a casualty dresser at the hospital. At last I decided that whatever the cost, and I knew it would be great, I would continue running competitively for two more years, provided I could still keep up with my medical studies.

I wanted to prove that my attitude towards training had been the right one, and hence restore the faith in myself that had been shaken by my Olympic defeat. I could accept being beaten in the Olympics—that had happened to many stronger favourites than me. What I objected to was that my defeat was taken by so many as proof that my way of training was wrong. I could not bear the thought that some other athlete might want to train along the lines that I had used, and that I might be held up as the bad example to dissuade him. This would happen unless I could bring myself to the sort of peak I felt capable of achieving.

My running had become something of a crusade. It was as if I were preaching about a special attitude towards running that I felt was right. It was a combination of the Greek approach I encountered at the Olympics, and of the University attitude that Oxford had taught me. I coupled this with my own love of running as one of the most perfect forms of physical expression. I believed that many other potential athletes could experience this same satisfaction. If my attitude were right then it should be possible to achieve great success, and I wanted to see this happen—either for myself or my friends.

182

Only in something like running can finality be achieved, the sort of finality that is almost perfection. But it is not the kind of perfection that leaves you with nothing to live for. You are not your own executioner, because sport is not the main aim in life. Yet to achieve perfection in one thing, however small, makes it possible to face uncertainty in the more difficult problems of life.

Throughout the winter of 1952-53 I stepped up the severity of my training programme by intensifying the interval method of running I have already described— Barthel used the same system. I had great admiration for him because he was not a semi-professional maintained by his country's government. He was a qualified chemist who did his training after his working day was over. He had shown that it was possible to reach the top and to do a normal day's work in addition.

In February and March I started track running, and would sometimes run as many as ten quarter-miles, each in about 63 seconds, and with an interval of two to three minutes between each. This was much more strenuous training than I had ever done before. It left me exhausted for several days, but it could be accomplished within the half-hour a day that I was able to spare for training.

There were to be no Olympic Games in 1953, no Empire Games, no European Games. In December 1952 John Landy of Australia, who had been knocked out in my heat at the Olympic Games, startled the world by running a mile in 4 min. 2.1 sec. This was the fastest mile in the world for seven years, and he followed it up with another in 4 min. 2.6 sec. I could hardly believe the improvement from the runner I had known at Helsinki. Landy made no secret of the fact that the four-minute mile was his goal. The race for the four-minute mile had really begun.

This was the goal that athletes and sportsmen had talked of and dreamt about for so many years, since the days of Paavo Nurmi, the great Finnish runner. Everyone used to think it was quite impossible, and beyond the reach of any runner. Then gradually the world mile record had been lowered:

|      |                        | Min. | Sec. |
|------|------------------------|------|------|
| 1922 | Nurmi, Finland .. .. .. | 4 | 10.4 |
| 1931 | Ladoumegue, France .. .. | 4 | 9.2 |
| 1933 | Lovelock, New Zealand .. | 4 | 7.6 |
| 1934 | Cunningham, U.S.A. .. .. | 4 | 6.8 |
| 1937 | Wooderson, Gt. Britain .. .. | 4 | 6.4 |
| 1942 | Haegg, Sweden .. .. .. | 4 | 6.2 |
| 1942 | Andersson, Sweden .. .. | 4 | 6.2 |
| 1942 | Haegg, Sweden .. .. .. | 4 | 4.6 |
| 1943 | Andersson, Sweden .. .. | 4 | 2.6 |
| 1944 | "          "       .. .. | 4 | 1.6 |
| 1945 | Haegg, Sweden .. .. .. | 4 | 1.4 |

It was the rivalry between Haegg and Andersson that brought the four-minute mile within sight.

Do records have any real importance? I sometimes

think that we would be better off without stop-watches so that no one would know how fast or slow a race was run. The important thing would be the struggle of one man against another for supremacy. Yet the time taken is important as a yardstick with which to assess the merit of the performance after the heat of the battle has died down.

Records are the bare bones of athletics, like numbers to a mathematician. Unless given a human touch they have no life, no appeal. Statisticians may juggle with them, some perhaps finding in their concentration on record figures a vicarious fulfilment of their own ambition. Like odds quoted on horses, times may tell you something of a man's chance of winning, but they can tell you nothing of his style or his length of stride, nor can a javelin thrower's distances tell you of his grace of throw. They can give you no conception of the joy there is in watching a champion athlete's supreme integration of movement, his genius at harnessing efficiently power that is partly inborn and partly ingrained by years of training. It is this human touch which makes the difference between the lasting excitement of men running and the temporary thrill of speedway or motor racing.

Just as the date of a wine is a guide to the connoisseur, so is knowledge of athletic records necessary for the true appraisal of a performance or for the prediction of a result. When kept in its place, an intimate knowledge of records can heighten the spectator's enjoyment and give the athlete an idea of his own relative standing in his sport. Victory or defeat can never quite give him this. He may be a large fish in a small pond, heading for a great shock when he first encounters the outside world in competition.

When I have to travel thousands of miles to meet well-publicised opponents, half the battle lies in knowing in advance the standard to expect, and in training to beat that standard. In the Olympic season I knew that I could not feel secure in winning races in Britain with 4 min. 9 sec. miles. I had to train with time trials that took me down to the equivalent of a 4 min. 3 sec. mile. Records should be the servants not the masters of the athlete, preparing him for a forthcoming encounter with a respected opponent. They should not be an end in themselves.

But what about the four-minute mile? At first I thought of this merely as a new record. It had no intrinsic merit, but was just a time like any other. By a strange coincidence it happened that the round figure of four minutes was just below the existing world record for the mile, and seemed to stand as a barrier to future progress in that event. Of course the four-minute mile would be important as a new record; but would it mean more than any other world record being broken?

The fact that public imagination had been captured, with the help of Press publicity, seemed to be irrelevant. After all, the time taken in a race merely depends on the way in which it happens to be run. The oxygen consumption of an athlete rises steeply as his speed increases. The miler is limited by lack of oxygen, and in order to keep his oxygen requirement to a minimum, would need to run at the slowest average speed to achieve his target of a four-minute mile—the ideal would be four even laps of sixty seconds each. If the time is the real object of the race, other competitors must be ignored, unless they co-operate wittingly or unwittingly, in the time schedule.

Wherever I went after John Landy's two races the inevitable question was broached. Was it possible for a man to run a mile in four minutes? To me the answer was obvious. Of course, as a result of more competition and better training, men would gradually run miles in faster and faster times, until four minutes was reached.

Nor would the progress stop there. For an improvement that cannot go on indefinitely there must be a limit. But rather as the tortoise in the mathematical problem, based on Æsop's fable, is never caught by the hare running at twice the speed, so the limit in miling would never be reached, although the margin by which the record was broken would continually diminish. To say, however, "Four minutes is only a time" was presumptuous, unless I had an answer for the inevitable follow-up question—"Well, if it's possible, why don't you do it?"

Whether as athletes we liked it or not, the four-minute

187

mile had become rather like an Everest—a challenge to the human spirit. It was a barrier that seemed to defy all attempts to break it—an irksome reminder that man's striving might be in vain. The Scandinavians, with their almost excessive reverence for the magic of sport, called it the "Dream Mile."

In the last few years there have been many more athletes practising in every country than ever before, and the standard in all athletic events has soared. Sprint records have always been paced—there has always been the incentive of a man at the winner's shoulder, and an improvement of less than 1 per cent in sprint performance cannot be measured by stop-watches, as it can in distance races. Sprinters do not greatly improve by new training methods, and so we have few new records.

For long distance races on the other hand, we are only just beginning to realise the amount of training the body can endure, and the improvement in performances has been meteoric, with new world records several times a year.

The mile race has had a strange history. It lies between sprints and long distance races. In 1953, despite many challenges, the world record set up by Gunder Haegg had stood for eight years. The mile—the Anglo-Saxon standard of distance—has captured the imagination of athletes and spectators alike in a way that its nearest metric equivalent, 1,500 metres, has never done. It was a popular event long before any one dreamt of the magic four minutes. It is a distance that seems to present a perfect test of judgment, speed and stamina.

After the gun there is a jockeying for a good position; then throughout the race there is the feeling of power being held in check, which provides continuous suspense, culminating in the uncertain climax of the finishing burst. Nowadays there is no lull or jog trot after the excitement of the first lap, and at the finish there is that possibility of surprise and daring that makes the result a gamble until the last stride.

If I entered the lists to attack the four-minute mile the problem was to decide how and where the race should be run. There were four essential requirements— a good track, absence of wind, warm weather and even-paced running. Some people have imagined that a four-minute mile might result from normal competition. This could only happen if there was an opponent capable of forcing the pace, right up to the last 50 yards. This was what Arne Andersson tried to do in 1945, to run Gunder Haegg off his feet, and to tire his finish. Gunder Haegg held out and was able to set up his own world record. Only John Landy could force me to a race of this kind, and by the time we ran against each other the four-minute mile might already have been accomplished, and it would be too late. It is easier to race an opponent than the clock, but I had no choice.

I had decided some years before that the Oxford track should be the scene of my attempt at the four-minute mile. The Oxford *v.* A.A.A. match provided the first opportunity of the 1953 season where I might expect suitable opposition in the early stages of the race. The biggest gamble was the weather, and I was taking a great chance in hoping for a suitable day in April.

My training was going well. At Easter I had taken a break from running and spent a long weekend climbing in North Wales. The sport of rock climbing was comparatively new to me, but its fascination already gripped me. In contrast to the all-out fury of running it provided a more critical, delicate approach. But after finding some laborious route to the summit it was always possible to run down the mountainside.

I remember a race down from the Snowdon Horseshoe with some friends. The wind sang in our ears and deafened us. Sometimes we tumbled, falling if we were lucky on a patch of grass, otherwise on hostile stones. We picked out likely landing places, as we jumped a ledge or boulder. Faster and faster we ran, each in turn leading until he slipped and was overtaken. Towards the bottom we could release ourselves from the agony of checking our descent, that tore at the overworked muscles of our thighs. It was a glorious moment when the level ground brought us under control.

At Penn-y-Pass we threw ourselves on the grass by a stream, and drank our fill of water. Then we rolled over on our backs and lay there, steamy perspiration rising from clothes that had been inadequate protection against the chill wind on the ridges. We had drunk too deeply of the dangerous mountain air, become too infatuated by the goddess of speed. Waiting to catch up with ourselves we rubbed our aching limbs, tired but happy.

I felt a different person on my return from Wales. I ran a ¾-mile trial on the 30th March, in 3 min. 1 sec., with three successive quarters each at the correct average speed for a four-minute mile, and then an 880 yards on 13th April in 1 min. 52.1 sec.—both unpaced. Shortly after, Chris Chataway, Walter Hasketh and I left for Morocco, where the wine was good and the competition would not be too severe. Our team was ably managed, as on many more important foreign tours, by Jack Crump of the British Amateur Athletic Board.

Walter Hasketh, the Lancashire cross-country runner, was the star of the tour. In his first race, accustomed to the freedom of the countryside, he was jostled, and crashed headlong on the track. The crowd gasped, as the other runners seemed to be trampling on him. He was yards behind as, streaming with blood, he looked furiously at the bunch of runners ahead. He climbed to his feet and courageously set off to catch them. Almost sprinting he overtook them all before his anger died down. Though he did not win, the crowd were delighted with his spirit and courage.

In all his subsequent races he was Morocco's hero, unmistakable as he ran, daubed with iodine from head to foot. At ceremonial banquets our team would be

191

called on for some entertainment. Walter, a juggler by profession, was always happy to oblige, using oranges, plates, bottles and anything else he could lay his hands on. With the Moroccans crying "Heskeeth," his light-fingered dexterity followed the last course of every meal.

The French principle of Colonial Government seemed to be to interfere as little as possible. The Moroccans, Berbers and Arabs believed apparently that Allah blesses those with the fewest wants, and spent a great deal of time just sitting or lying down. Perhaps they had had a surfeit of ambition, power, warfare and booty in past generations. Compared with Turkey there was much less "westernisation." Many habits and customs could not have changed for a thousand years, during which sultans and caliphs rapidly succeeded each other as they were poisoned by their wives or decapitated by their rivals.

When I ran at Oxford on 2nd May 1953, a week after my return from Morocco, I aimed at breaking Sydney Wooderson's British mile record of 4 min. 6.4 sec. which had stood ever since he set it up in a handicap race at Motspur Park on 28th August 1937. R. H. Thomas, a well-known miler of the time, started level with him and attempted to pace him for ¾-mile. There were other runners with up to 250 yards, start to help him in the later stages. This may seem far removed from the conditions of an ordinary race, but it was the only approach open to him, because there was no runner in Europe at the time who could have extended him.

192

Chris Chataway was also running for the A.A.A. in the match at Oxford on 2nd May, and he agreed to run as hard as he could for the first ¾-mile. It was our first attempt to run four even quarters and our lap times were 61.7, 62.4, 61.1 sec. Then I went into the lead and ran a last lap of 58.4 sec. to give a total time of 4 min. 3.6 sec., a new British record. We ran the first half-mile too slowly to come near the four-minute mile, but we were delighted to have done so well in a first attempt. This race made me realise that the four-minute mile was not out of reach. It was only a question of time; but would someone else reach the goal first?

Every time after this when I ran on the track the public and Press expected new records. On 6th May there was a 4 × 1,500 metres relay attack at Leyton on the world record by the Achilles Club represented by Law, Brasher, Chataway and myself. We failed to beat the world record, but our combined time of 15 min. 49.6 sec. bettered the best time ever made by a British four, at Cologne in 1931, by 6 seconds.

On 16th May I ran in a special invitation ¾-mile on the exposed Wimbledon track. There was a gale blowing, and I knew a record was out of the question. I did not wish to disappoint everyone, and ran a ¾-mile in 2 min. 59.8 sec. Because of the wind this effort exhausted me more than my recent Oxford mile.

The British Games mile at the White City at Whitsun, on 23rd May, was also described as a record at-

193

tempt. The Press technique had become something like this. If Smith has entered for a race they can get two headlines out of it; first, "Smith to attack world record," even though Smith disclaims any such intention. If the record is not broken, their second headline is all ready, "Smith fails in world record bid." The feelings of Smith about this would be interesting but perhaps unprintable. It does no harm, I suppose, so long as the public and Smith do not take it too seriously.

I won this international mile race at the White City in 4 min. 9.4 sec., with a last lap of 56.6 sec. I considered that to win would be enough, as in the old days when there was no question of a record. But this result was greeted with a headline, "Bannister held back so it looked a race."

I would have attempted the mile record at Oxford on 30th May in a match for London University, but the wind was hopelessly strong. I ran a half-mile instead in 1 min. 51.9 sec., a ground and meeting record.

A week later I was attempting to increase my speed by quarter-miling at the Middlesex Championships at Edmonton. I covered the first bend at a speed exceptional for me. Just as I was overtaking a runner in an outside lane I felt a twang in my left thigh as sharp as a violin string snapping, and limped off the track. I had "pulled" a muscle for the first time.

I had been running too fast for my muscles, which were unaccustomed to sprinting at this speed. Until

194

then I had never been able to understand how athletes pulled muscles. Now it was all too clear. In the next hour the pain grew worse. I had chosen the worst possible moment, because on the same day Wes Santee in America threw out a new challenge with a mile in 4 min. 2.4 sec. How soon could I recover and make another attempt?

After a day or two I realised that the "pull" was not as serious as I feared. The muscle fibres were probably not torn, but a small blood vessel supplying them might have burst, which would have made the muscle seize up. M. M. Mays, the A.A.A. masseur, skilfully dispersed the adhesions after I had rested the leg for five days. In eight days I was dancing, and after ten days I was running gently.

In the middle of the following week, after nothing but slow running since the injury, I was able to run two half-miles in under two minutes each. This meant that I could run at the speed of a four-minute mile without aggravating the injury. An enthusiastic friend persuaded me that I ought to run a paced time trial.

To avoid Press excitement in case my pulled muscle did not hold out, the event was secretly included as a special invitation race in the Surrey Schools athletic meeting at Motspur Park on the following Saturday, 27th June. I had no idea what would happen, or whether I could last out the distance. I only knew that the same afternoon 5 hours later, Wes Santee was to run in Dayton, Ohio, and was confidently predicting a four-minute mile.

I was uncertain how I was to be paced, but Don Mac-Millan, the Australian Olympic runner, led for 2½ laps. Then Chris Brasher, who had run the first two laps at snail's pace, loomed on the horizon in front of me, but a lap in arrear. He proceeded to encourage me by shouting backwards over his shoulder as he ran ahead of me, just preventing himself from being lapped.

All things considered it could hardly be called a race. I accept full responsibility for running in it, though I did not organise the details. My lap times were 59.6, 60.1, 62.1 and 60.2 sec., making a total time of 4 min. 2 sec. This was the third fastest mile of all time, beaten only by Haegg and Andersson eight years before. My feeling as I look back is one of great relief that I did not run a four-minute mile under such artificial circumstances.

Immediately after the run Chris Brasher and I drove off to North Wales. That night we were sleeping in a hay loft under a skylight and looking forward to a day of climbing. Next morning we sat sunbathing on a flat-topped pinnacle in the Welsh mountains, blissfully unaware of the reaction in Fleet Street to our Motspur Park effort. The general Press opinion was perhaps best summed up by *The Times* correspondent:

"The profound secrecy with which the project was planned and carried out—and it certainly was an ingenious, if slightly odd, idea to pitchfork so important an event into a school children's meeting—prevented all but a favoured few from being able to give an eye-witness account. How far the secrecy really assisted Bannister as a great athlete unavoidably in the public eye, and all that means, seems open to question. How, too, it will assist British athletics as a whole is not clear.

Nor is one quite sure about the motive behind the secrecy. Some will think Bannister, at the start at any rate, was concerned mainly with testing more or less in private the muscle he pulled a few weeks ago. Or he may have been seriously intent upon the exceptional time he in fact achieved without any preliminary speculation on the subject. Or, if one dare suggest such a thing, he may even have had the four-minute mile itself in mind. Doubtless also there was the knowledge that almost simultaneously W. Santee, the American who recently started the world by doing the distance in 4 min. 2.4 sec., was having another go . . .

Public interest seems to demand some kind of explanation of so important an effort."

A report of the race, "so far as one has gathered from a kindly spy," followed.

This was my last deliberate attempt of the season. On the same day Santee, under the full glare of publicity, made his attempt to run the four-minute mile, and took 4 min. 7.6 sec. I could only hope that he would not forestall me before the end of his season.

On 12th July the British Amateur Athletic Board ratified my 4 min. 3.6 sec. mile run at Oxford on 2nd May as a British all-comers' and British national record. On

197

my 4 min. 2 sec. mile run at Motspur Park on 27th June the Board issued a statement:

"The Board, having very carefully considered the circumstances connected with this performance, regret that, although it has no doubt that the time was accomplished, it cannot recognise the performance as a record.

It has been compelled to take this action because it does not consider the event was a *bona fide* competition according to the rules. The Board wishes it to be known that whilst appreciating the public enthusiasm for record performances, and the natural and commendable desire of athletes to accomplish them, it does not regard individual record attempts as in the best interest of athletics as a whole."

The news of the rejection of my 4 min. 2 sec. mile for record purposes brought journalists flocking to the family door-step. "What are your views about it?" they asked, feeling they were on the brink of a sensation. "No comment?" they pleaded. "Surely you must have some views on it? Will you appeal? Only say yes or no!" "No comment," I repeated. To add a single sentence was dangerous. Anything said could be twisted. "Bannister will not appeal," is as good a headline as "Bannister will appeal," when a story is "hot." If I were once tempted into the slightest utterance further amplification would be called for, and I should find myself in deeper and deeper waters. I stuck to "No comment," instead, and evaded all questions. My own inner feelings were that I accepted the decision without question. I had never

198

expected the record to be ratified. There was really nothing important at stake. If the time *had* been under four minutes, the fat would really have been in the fire.

After this "irregular" attempt I realised two things. In the first place only two painful seconds now separated me from the four-minute mile, and I was certain that I could cut down the time. The second point was that I knew the attempt would be meaningless unless it were achieved in a *bona fide* race, in which all runners set out to finish, although the lead might be shared at different stages by the various competitors in order to ensure a fast even pace. I decided that unless these conditions could be fulfilled I would rather not make the attempt.

For the rest of the season I forgot all about records. Two weeks later on 11th July I won the 1953 A.A.A. mile championship in 4 min. 5.2 sec., the fastest time for the meeting. After this I was too busy studying to be able to do any serious training, though on 1st August I ran a 4 min. 7.6 mile in a 4 × 1 mile relay attempt on the world record. Our team included Chataway, Nankeville and Seaman, and I ran last without any competition from the other team. Our combined time was 16 min. 41 sec. and it was good enough to beat the previous world record of 16 min. 42.8 sec., set up by a Swedish team on 5th August 1949. It was well within the previous British National Record of 16 min. 53.2 sec., made on 4th August 1952 when I co-operated in a British Empire team with Landy, Law and Parnell. Two days later, on August Bank Holiday, I ran my fastest half-mile, 1 min. 50.7 sec., against El Mabrouk of France.

Soon it was the end of our season and of the American too. But in Australia the season was just opening, and I waited anxiously for news of John Landy, who was getting into his stride there. This would be his second season devoted to record-breaking runs, and I felt that it was only a question of time before he ran a four-minute mile.

Landy preferred running out in front to having a pacemaker, and the warmer climate of Australia was more favourable for his efforts. Landy is a year younger than I, and did not begin to improve as a runner until 1951, when he reduced his mile time to 4 min. 15.2 sec., running behind Don MacMillan.

His training programme was probably more severe than any other middle distance runner's in the world. It involved weight lifting and running every day to a total of 200 miles a month. Percy Cerutty, at one time Landy's coach, has said that Landy has the temperament of a fanatic. He does not consider this a term of disparagement but the highest possible praise to accord to any man. The three runners he considers to have had it are Nurmi, Zatopek and Landy.

John Landy is reported to have commented that when his daily mileage was released to the world it would show that he had covered greater distances than any other first class runner, with the exception of Emil Zatopek. By December 1953 John Landy had embarked on a course

of training that was in the 20-miles-a-session class. He
opened with a 4 min. 2 sec. mile on a grass track in December—a great performance, 0.1 of a second faster than
his best of the previous year.

But something was wrong. His harder training and
selfless expenditure of himself brought no improvement.
Each week I waited for the news of his times. The tension grew as at each attempt he narrowly missed his target. By April 1954 he had won six races all in times less
than 4 min. 3 sec., a record achieved by no other athlete
in history. Each race, incidentally, was headlined in the
British newspapers as "Landy fails." If this was failure,
was what the meaning of success? After one race in
February he lost heart. "It's a brick wall," he said. "I
shall not attempt it again." But he had caught the four-
minute fever, and was already planning a summer in
Scandinavia, where the tracks are perfect and the climate
such that he could make repeated attempts.

Landy's personality intrigued me. I was dependent
solely on the comments of Percy Cerutty, the Australian
coach, who said he had seen in Landy "demonstrations
of a character capable of the greatest kindness, gentle-
ness and thoughtfulness, and on the other side—as there
is and always must be—a ruthlessness, lack of feeling for
others, and a ferocity and antagonism, albeit it is mostly
vented on himself, that makes it possible on occasions
for John to rise to sublime heights of physical endeavour."

201

If all this were true, he was indeed a formidable opponent. I wondered what would happen when we met. His solo record-breaking running was only the prelude to the duel between us that was bound to come, provided all went well and we were both selected for the Empire Games at Vancouver in 1954.

# CHAPTER FOURTEEN

# FOUR-MINUTE MILE

## 1954

*"Now bid me run,*
*And I will strive with things impossible."*
JULIUS CAESAR.

I EXPECTED that the summer of 1954 would be my last competitive season. It was certain to be a big year in athletics. There would be the Empire Games in Vancouver, the European Games in Berne, and hopes were running high of a four-minute mile.

The great change that now came over my running was that I no longer trained and raced alone. Perhaps I had mellowed a little and was becoming more sociable. Every day between 12.30 and 1.30 I trained on a track in Paddington and had a quick lunch before returning to hospital. We called ourselves the Paddington lunch time club. We came from all parts of London and our common bond was a love of running.

I felt extremely happy in the friendships I made there, as we shared the hard work of repetitive quarter miles and sprints. These training sessions came to mean almost as much to me as had those at the Oxford track.

203

I could now identify myself more intimately with the failure and success of other runners.

In my hardest training Chris Brasher was with me, and he made the task very much lighter. On Friday evenings he took me along to Chelsea Barracks where his coach, Franz Stampfl, held a training session. At weekends Chris Chataway would join us, and in this friendly atmosphere the very severe training we did became most enjoyable.

In December 1953 we started a new intensive course of training and ran several times a week a series of ten consecutive quarter-miles, each in 66 seconds. Through January and February we gradually speeded them up, keeping to an interval of two minutes between each. By April we could manage them in 61 seconds, but however hard we tried it did not seem possible to reach our target of 60 seconds. We were stuck, or as Chris Brasher expressed it—"bogged down." The training had ceased to do us any good and we needed a change.

Chris Brasher and I drove up to Scotland overnight for a few days' climbing. We turned into the Pass of Glencoe as the sun crept above the horizon at dawn. A misty curtain drew back from the mountains and the "sun's sleepless eye" cast a fresh cold light on the world. The air was calm and fragrant, and the colours of sunrise were mirrored in peaty pools on the moor. Soon the sun was up and we were off climbing. The weekend was a complete mental and physical change. It probably did us more harm than good physically. We climbed hard for the four days we were there, using the wrong muscles in slow and jerking movements.

There was an element of danger too. I remember Chris falling a short way when leading a climb up a rock face depressingly named "Jericho's Wall." Luckily he did not hurt himself. We were both worried lest a sprained ankle might set our training back by several weeks.

After three days our minds turned to running again. We suddenly became alarmed at the thought of taking any more risks, and decided to return. We had slept little, our meals had been irregular. But when we tried to run those quarter-miles again, the time came down to 59 seconds!

It was now less than three weeks to the Oxford University *v.* A.A.A. race, the first opportunity of the year for us to attack the four-minute mile. Chris Chataway had decided to join Chris Brasher and myself in the A.A.A. team. He doubted his ability to run a ¾-mile in three minutes, but he generously offered to attempt it.

I had now abandoned the severe training of the previous months and was concentrating entirely on gaining speed and freshness. I had to learn to release in four short minutes the energy I usually spent in half an hour's training. Each training session took on a special significance, as the day of the Oxford race drew near. It felt a privilege and joy each time I ran a trial on the track.

There was no longer any need for my mind to force my limbs to run faster—my body became a unity in mo-

205

tion much greater than the sum of its component parts. I never thought of length of stride or style, or even my judgment of pace. All this had become automatically ingrained. In this way a singleness of drive could be achieved, leaving my mind free from the task of directing operations so that it could fix itself on the great objective ahead. There was more enjoyment in my running than ever before, a new health and vigour. It was as if all my muscles were a part of a perfectly tuned machine. I felt fresh now at the end of each training session.

On 24th April I ran a ¾-mile trial in three minutes at Motspur Park with Chataway. I led for the first two laps and we both returned exactly the same time. Four days later I ran a last solo ¾-mile trial at Paddington. Norris McWhirter, who had been my patient timekeeper through most of 1953, came over to hold the watch.

The energy of the twins, Norris and Ross McWhirter, was boundless. For them nothing was too much trouble, and they accepted any challenge joyfully. After running together in Oxford as sprinters they carried their partnership into journalism, keeping me posted of the performances of my overseas rivals. They often drove me to athletics meetings, so that I arrived with no fuss, never a minute too soon or too late. Sometimes I was not sure whether it was Norris or Ross who held the watch or drove the car, but I knew that either could be relied upon.

For the trial at Paddington there was as usual a high wind blowing. I would have given almost anything to be able to shirk the test that would tell me with ruthless accuracy what my chances were of achieving a four-minute mile at Oxford. I felt that 2 min. 59.9 sec. for the ¾-mile in a solo training run meant 3 min. 59.9 sec. in a mile race. A time of 3 min. 0.1 sec. would mean 4 min. 0.1 sec. for the mile—just the difference between success and failure. The watch recorded a time of 2 min. 59.9 sec.! I felt a little sick afterwards and had the taste of nervousness in my mouth. My speedy recovery within five minutes suggested that I had been holding something back. Two days later at Paddington I ran a 1 min. 54 sec. half-mile quite easily, after a late night, and then took five days complete rest before the race.

I had been training daily since the previous November, and now that the crisis was approaching I barely knew what to do with myself. I spent most of the time imagining I was developing a cold and wondering if the gale-force winds would ever drop. The day before the race I slipped on a highly polished hospital floor and spent the rest of the day limping. Each night in the week before the race there came a moment when I saw myself at the starting line. My whole body would grow nervous and tremble. I ran the race over in my mind. Then I would calm myself and sometimes get off to sleep.

Next day was Thursday, 6th May 1954. I went into the hospital as usual, and at 11 o'clock I was sharpening my spikes on a grindstone in the laboratory. Someone passing said, "You don't really think that's going to make any difference, do you?"

207

I knew the weather conditions made the chances of success practically nil. Yet all day I was taking the usual precautions for the race, feeling at the same time that they would prove useless.

I decided to travel up to Oxford alone because I wanted to think quietly. I took an early train deliberately, opened a carriage door, and, quite by chance, there was Franz Stampfl inside. I was delighted to see him, as a friend with the sort of attractive cheerful personality I badly needed at that moment. Through Chris Brasher, Franz had been in touch with my training programme, but my own connection with him was slight.

I would have liked his advice and help at this moment, but could not bring myself to ask him. It was as if now, at the end of my running career, I was being forced to admit that coaches were necessary after all, and that I had been wrong to think that the athlete could be sufficient unto himself.

In my mind there lurked the memory of an earlier occasion when I had visited a coach. He had expounded his views on my running and suggested a whole series of changes. The following week I read a newspaper article he wrote about my plans, claiming to be my adviser for the 1952 Olympics. This experience made me inclined to move slowly.

But Franz is not like this. He has no wish to turn the athlete into a machine working at his dictation. We shared a common view of athletics as a means of "recreation" of each individual, as a result of the liberation

208

and expression of the latent power within him. Franz is an artist who can see beauty in human struggle and achievement.

We talked, almost impersonally, about the problem I faced. In my mind I had settled this as the day when, with every ounce of strength I possessed, I would attempt to run the four-minute mile. A wind of gale force was blowing which would slow me up by a second a lap. In order to succeed I must run not merely a four-minute mile, but the equivalent of a 3 min. 56 sec. mile in calm weather.

I had reached my peak physically and psychologically. There would never be another day like it. I had to drive myself to the limit of my power without the stimulus of competitive opposition. This was my first race for eight months and all this time I had been storing nervous energy. If I tried and failed I should be dejected, and my chances would be less on any later attempt. Yet it seemed that the high wind was going to make it impossible.

I had almost decided when I entered the carriage at Paddington that unless the wind dropped soon I would postpone the attempt. I would just run an easy mile in Oxford and make the attempt on the next possible occasion—ten days later at the White City in London.

Franz understood my apprehension. He thought I was capable of running a mile in 3 min. 56 sec., or 3.57, so he could argue convincingly that it was worth while making the attempt. "With the proper motivation, that is, a good reason for wanting to do it," he said, "your mind can overcome any sort of adversity. In any case the wind might drop. I remember J. J. Barry in Ireland. He ran a 4 min. 8 sec. mile without any training or even proper food—simply because he had the will to run. Later in America where he was given every facility and encouragement, he never ran a fast race. In any case, what if this were your only chance?"

He had won his point. Racing has always been more of a mental than a physical problem to me. He went on talking about athletes and performances, but I heard no more. The dilemma was not banished from my mind, and the idea left uppermost was that this might be my only chance. "How would you ever forgive yourself if you rejected it?" I thought, as the train arrived in Oxford. As it happened, ten days later it was just as windy!

I was met at the station by Charles Wenden, a great friend from my early days in Oxford, who drove me straight down to Iffley Road. The wind was almost gale force. Together we walked round the deserted track. The St. George's flag on a nearby church stood out from the flagpole. The attempt seemed hopeless, yet for some unknown reason I tried out both pairs of spikes. I had a new pair which were specially made for me on the instructions of a climber and fell walker, Eustace Thomas of Manchester. Some weeks before he had come up to London and together we worked out modifications which would reduce the weight of each running shoe from six to four ounces. This saving in weight might well mean the difference between success and failure.

Still undecided, I drove back to Charles Wenden's home for lunch. On this day, as on many others, I was glad of the peace which I found there. Although both he and his wife Eileen knew the importance of the decision that had to be made, and cared about it as much as I did myself, it was treated by common consent as a question to be settled later.

The immediate problem was to prepare a suitable lunch, and to see that the children, Felicity and Sally, ate theirs. Absorbed in watching the endless small routine of running a home and family, I could forget some of my apprehensions. Charles Wenden had been one of the ex-service students in Oxford after the war, and some of my earliest running had been in his company. Later his house had become a second home for me during my research studies in Oxford, and the calm efficiency of Eileen had often helped to still my own restless worries. Never was this factor so important as on this day.

In the afternoon I called on Chris Chataway. At the moment the sun was shining, and he lay stretched on the window seat. He smiled and said, just as I knew he would, "The day could be a lot worse, couldn't it? Just now it's fine. The forecast says the wind may drop towards evening. Let's not decide until five o'clock."

I spent the afternoon watching from the window the swaying of the leaves. "The wind's hopeless," said Joe Binks on the way down to the track. At 5.15 there was

221

a shower of rain. The wind blew strongly, but now came in gusts, as if uncertain. As Brasher, Chataway and I warmed up, we knew the eyes of the spectators were on us; they were hoping that the wind would drop just a little—if not enough to run a four-minute mile, enough to make the attempt.

Failure is as exciting to watch as success, provided the effort is absolutely genuine and complete. But the spectators fail to understand—and how can they know—the mental agony through which an athlete must pass before he can give his maximum effort. And how rarely, if he is built as I am, he can give it.

No one tried to persuade me. The decision was mine alone, and the moment was getting closer. As we lined up for the start I glanced at the flag again. It fluttered more gently now, and the scene from Shaw's *Saint Joan* flashed through my mind, how she, at her desperate moment, waited for the wind to change. Yes, the wind was dropping slightly. This was the moment when I made my decision. The attempt was on.

There was complete silence on the ground . . . a false start . . . I felt angry that precious moments during the lull in the wind might be slipping by. The gun fired a second time. . . . Brasher went into the lead and I slipped in effortlessly behind him, feeling tremendously full of running. My legs seemed to meet no resistance at all, as if propelled by some unknown force.

We seemed to be going so slowly! Impatiently I

212

shouted "Faster!" But Brasher kept his head and did not change the pace. I went on worrying until I heard the first lap time, 57.5 sec. In the excitement my knowledge of pace had deserted me. Brasher could have run the first quarter in 55 seconds without my realising it, because I felt so full of running, but I should have had to pay for it later. Instead, he had made success possible.

At one and a half laps I was still worrying about the pace. A voice shouting "relax" penetrated to me above the noise of the crowd. I learnt afterwards it was Stampfl's. Unconsciously I obeyed. If the speed was wrong it was too late to do anything about it, so why worry? I was relaxing so much that my mind seemed almost detached from my body. There was no strain.

I barely noticed the half-mile, passed in 1 min. 58 sec., nor when, round the next bend, Chataway went into the lead. At three-quarters of a mile the effort was still barely perceptible; the time was 3 min. 0.7 sec., and by now the crowd was roaring. Somehow I had to run that last lap in 59 seconds. Chataway led round the next bend and then I pounced past him at the beginning of the back straight, three hundred yards from the finish.

I had a moment of mixed joy and anguish, when my mind took over. It raced well ahead of my body and drew my body compellingly forward. I felt that the moment of a lifetime had come. There was no pain, only a great unity of movement and aim. The world seemed to stand still, or did not exist. The only reality

213

was the next two hundred yards of track under my feet. The tape meant finality—extinction perhaps.

I felt at that moment that it was my chance to do one thing supremely well. I drove on, impelled by a combination of fear and pride. The air I breathed filled me with the spirit of the track where I had run my first race. The noise in my ears was that of the faithful Oxford crowd. Their hope and encouragement gave me greater strength. I had now turned the last bend and there were only fifty yards more.

My body had long since exhausted all its energy, but it went on running just the same. The physical overdraft came only from greater willpower. This was the crucial moment when my legs were strong enough to carry me over the last few yards as they could never have done in previous years. With five yards to go the tape seemed almost to recede. Would I ever reach it?

Those last few seconds seemed never-ending. The faint line of the finishing tape stood ahead as a haven of peace, after the struggle. The arms of the world were waiting to receive me if only I reached the tape without slackening my speed. If I faltered, there would be no arms to hold me and the world would be a cold, forbidding place, because I had been so close. I leapt at the tape like a man taking his last spring to save himself from the chasm that threatens to engulf him.

My effort was over and I collapsed almost unconscious, with an arm on either side of me. It was only

214

then that real pain overtook me. I felt like an exploded flashlight with no will to live; I just went on existing in the most passive physical state without being quite unconscious. Blood surged from my muscles and seemed to fell me. It was as if all my limbs were caught in an ever-tightening vice. I knew that I had done it before I even heard the time. I was too close to have failed, unless my legs had played strange tricks at the finish by slowing me down and not telling my tiring brain that they had done so.

The stop-watches held the answer. The announcement came—"Result of one mile . . . time, 3 minutes" —the rest lost in the roar of excitement. I grabbed Brasher and Chataway, and together we scampered round the track in a burst of spontaneous joy. We had done it—the three of us!

We shared a place where no man had yet ventured— secure for all time, however fast men might run miles in future. We had done it where we wanted, when we wanted, how we wanted, in our first attempt of the year. In the wonderful joy my pain was forgotten and I wanted to prolong those precious moments of realisation.

I felt suddenly and gloriously free of the burden of athletic ambition that I had been carrying for years. No words could be invented for such supreme happiness, eclipsing all other feelings. I thought at that moment I could never again reach such a climax of single-minded-

215

ness. I felt bewildered and overpowered. I knew it would be some time before I caught up with myself.

I was to meet the Chrises in London later, and I travelled up by car for a television programme. My companions were amazed that I could sit so silently, not looking either excited or happy. If only they knew how happy I was! I was resting on billowy white clouds that would, I thought then, always protect me from the worst of life's buffetings. I felt that my defeat at Helsinki had been wiped out.

We had an evening of celebration. We learnt later that the news leaked through to the Oxford Union, where a member moved the adjournment of the House for 3 min. 59.4 sec. The new Indian President of the Union was confused. He refused to accept the motion because "notice had not been given."

The Press were on my trail everywhere all next day. To avoid their attentions I could only reach and leave my home through the garden with the help of chairs and ladders over a succession of fences. I escaped to Oxford for a quiet day with my friends the Wendens. When I returned to London I needed a suitcase to carry off my telegrams and letters. It was the beginning of a fan mail and of invitations to open bazaars that have continued ever since.

On the following Monday the Foreign Office asked me to get in touch with them. The British Information Services had suggested to them that I should come to

216

New York to make television and sound broadcasts of a "goodwill" nature. To me it seemed the strangest of missions, but who was I to question the wisdom of the Foreign Office?

Fearing complications, I made several stipulations—that I was only accepting the invitation at the request of the Foreign Office, that it must be made clear in advance that I did not intend to run in the United States, and that any fees received would be given to charity. Knowing nothing more about the organisation of my mission I arrived at the B.O.A.C. Air Terminal and was met by a Foreign Office official. He told me that an American broadcasting company had requested that I should travel secretly so that I could make a surprise appearance in a programme when I arrived. It grew "curiouser and curiouser."

The Foreign Office representative said that someone had already recognised me, and he would take me to the Foreign Office until I had to leave for the plane. They soon realised that it was impossible to keep my visit secret. There was a Press release in London, and a Press conference at London Airport before I left.

The big treatment was waiting for me as soon as I arrived in New York—a police escort from the plane included. The welcome was tremendous. I stood in front of television and newsreel cameras for about half an hour, answering questions and talking about British athletics and the four-minute mile. I had to answer any questions they shot at me, even one that nearly stunned me—"Do you expect to be knighted?"

A Press conference followed, and with the head of British Information Services at my side, I tried to answer questions fired as the second discharge of their welcoming salvo—

"Why are you here?"

"Isn't it more usual for athletes to run than to travel three thousand miles to appear on television?"

"Are you aware that you travelled under the false name of Richard Bentley?"

"Do you know who sponsored your trip?"

At this point a man who had been in favour of whisking me off as soon as I arrived, and had looked increasingly troubled throughout, sprang to his feet—

"I am the producer of the television programme, 'I've got a secret,' sponsored by a tobacco company. We invited Bannister over here, paid his fare, and chose the name Richard Bentley."

It was the first I had heard of any of this. "Do you approve of smoking?" the Press asked. Then the question of endangering my amateur status was raised, and the fun began. The head of the British Information Services came to my rescue. He explained that he was in consultation with Jack Crump of the British A.A.A. and Dan Ferris of the American A.A.A., so that my amateur status would not be endangered. For my own protection I was taken away to stay with the British Consul General's family in New York.

218

This confusion was most unfortunate. It made it more difficult for me to fulfil the purpose of my visit. After a day the uproar subsided, and I was able to go ahead with a series of unsponsored broadcasts and television interviews, which the British Information Services arranged for me, covering almost every network in the United States.

The problem of my amateur status was raised again two days later when a representative of the Olympic Committee of Southern California arrived in New York. He had brought a most expensive trophy to be awarded to the first man to run a mile in four minutes, whatever his country. In advertising that the trophy was worth three hundred dollars they had not bargained for the Press looking up the amateur rules. These limited the value of any prize an athlete might receive to twelve pounds sterling! We were off again!

Eventually I was presented with a replica worth the exact maximum possible. I returned the original, which I was not allowed to keep, for annual competition by milers in the United States, and they decided to rename the trophy the Bannister Award. An apt comment on the whole mix-up was made in the Oxford Union a week later—"You can hardly give a girl a bunch of flowers nowadays without endangering her amateur status."

When my official duties were over I had time for relaxation. There were parties, and one new experience— a tour of New York by helicopter, which skirted skyscrapers, flew under bridges, and hovered round the Statue of Liberty like an irreverent insect.

The most persistent criticism of the organisation of my visit to New York came from one section of the British Press. Their correspondents even approached me to ask how much money I had in my pockets and what allowance I had been given!

After four days of this excitement I arrived back in England and gave an account to the Foreign Office. A question was asked in the House of Commons on Monday, 17th May. Mr. Selwyn Lloyd's reply was:

"The British Information Services, New York, were asked by a producer of programmes to transmit an invitation to Mr. Bannister to appear on television. The Foreign Office were glad to ask Mr. Bannister to accept this invitation as it was felt that nothing but good to Anglo-American relations would result. At the time it was thought that no difficulties over Mr. Bannister's amateur status would arise from his undertaking a visit from which he himself would receive no personal gain.

"After arrangements had been made for Mr. Bannister's journey, some doubt arose on the ground that his appearance was to be on a sponsored programme. The rules on status vary from sport to sport (and appear about as complicated as those relating to offices of profit under the Crown). In the circumstances, it was decided that it would be wiser for him not to appear in that particular programme. Her Majesty's Government have assumed full financial responsibility for his visit.

"The visit has been an outstanding success. I have a long list with me of the various radio and television ap-

220

pearances which he made, and his other public engagements. He received a great welcome in New York and says he thoroughly enjoyed his visit, and I am sure that it has been a very good thing for Anglo-American relations."

Yes, "he thoroughly enjoyed his visit."

# CHAPTER FIFTEEN

# EMPIRE GAMES

## VANCOUVER 1954

*"For the race is run by one and one,*
*And never by two and two."*
                KIPLING.

MY FOUR-MINUTE MILE was secure, but it was only a question of time before John Landy from Australia, or Wes Santee from America, broke the barrier too, perhaps lowering my record as well. We had proved in Oxford that the four-minute mile was possible, and now the progress would continue. Landy, in search of ideal record breaking conditions, arrived in Finland soon after my Oxford run. His first attempt took 4 min. 1.6 sec., and I waited expectantly for even better times.

Meanwhile my own running was in the doldrums. It was the inevitable reaction after the four-minute mile and the inactivity of my whirlwind visit to New York. When I attempted to run a fast half mile on the Saturday before Whitsun in the British Games at the White City, I completely misjudged my fitness.

Eager to improve my speed, I had rushed into sprinting immediately I resumed training. I could not raise a challenge when Jungwirth of Czechoslavakia shot past me in the final straight. Though it was my second fastest half-mile, my time of 1 min. 51.3 sec. disappointed me. I accepted defeat with resignation, the result of the anti-climax after Oxford.

On Whit-Monday I ran in the International two-mile race, hoping to be able to pace Chris Chataway in a world record attempt. I was leading at the mile in 4 min. 20 sec., but then my legs seized up completely with stiffness. I had never run any distances above a mile on the track—I had become over-specialised. Struggling hard I fell right back from the leaders and finished sixth. I was very disappointed that I could not help Chris more. He missed the world record by a most unlucky fraction of a second.

Then one day Chris surprised me by saying he had decided to go to Finland to race against John Landy. I said I felt certain that this would provide Landy with the stimulus he was so obviously needing. In Finland he had already run four races close to the four minute mile, but he still seemed unable to cut down the last 2 seconds.

Chris thought there must be something wrong with a runner who could break 4 min. 3 sec. so many times and yet not get below four minutes, even under Scandinavian conditions. He thought he might beat Landy, who was believed to have no finishing burst, by hanging on and sprinting past him in the final straight. At the

223

time, quite humanly I think, I was a little upset at the thought that in the process Landy might break my own record.

So, after having pulled me from in front at Oxford, Chris went to Finland and pushed Landy from behind at Turku. They raced on 22nd June, and weather conditions were ideal. Landy led after the first lap. He glanced behind him at the bell, and seeing Chris on his heels took fright as he had never done during his solo runs. Almost for the first time, under the stimulus of real competition, he unleashed a tremendous finish, which at last brought him below four minutes. He set up a magnificent new world record of 3 min. 58 sec.

I was waiting for the news at home and heard the first announcement. For a few minutes I was stunned. The margin of 1.4 sec. by which he had broken my record was even greater than anything I had feared.

Until this shock I was easing off my training and had no incentive to run. The moment I heard the news my whole attitude changed. The comment I made to the Press half an hour later was that I was glad that Landy had broken the barrier too. I told them I had cabled him my heartiest congratulations. He had tried harder than anyone and I felt happy for him that he had succeeded. As far as the new world record was concerned, records were made to be broken. Men would go on breaking records as long as they ran. There was no limit. I had only held the world record for 46 days.

Landy, not Santee, had now become my rival. Wes Santee had, however, come very near to achieving the four-minute mile. On 29th May his time came down to 4 min. 1.3 sec. at Kansas City. Then followed two remarkable runs within a single week. On 4th and 11th June he achieved the fantastic pair of times 4 min. 0.6 sec. and 4 min. 0.7 sec., before he was removed from the sphere of immediate competition for service in the U.S. Marines. His run on 4th June was at that time the second fastest mile in history.

The real struggle between Landy and myself now began. In six weeks we were to race against each other in the Empire Games in Vancouver. The four-minute mile, however final and perfect it had seemed at Oxford, now meant nothing unless I could defeat John Landy. The Empire Games title had become more important to me than the four-minute mile, and more important to John Landy than the world record. I now felt grateful to Chataway for having gone to Finland and given me this great new incentive.

Running was a gamble. Over the years I had played for higher and higher stakes. The four-minute mile was the greatest bid I had ever made, and at the time I thought there was no answer. Now John Landy had gone one better. One race did not settle everything, as I had thought it would.

One race is only the prelude to another. Neither John Landy nor myself—nor the general public—could tol-

225

erate the kind of stalemate set up by our two records having been made away from each other. The world seemed almost too small for us and we must meet to settle the score.

Tactical plans for big races have to be thought out in advance. The runner must be prepared both to meet possible moves by an opponent and to retain the flexibility to modify his scheme if something happens quite unexpectedly. The simpler such plans can be, the better, because then the mind can be free during the race. This makes it easier to relax and run more economically.

My plans were extremely simple. I had to force John Landy to set the pace of a four-minute mile for me, rather as Arne Andersson had done for Gunder Haegg in 1945. I must reserve my effort of will power for the moment when I would fling myself past him near the finish. Until then I would be entirely passive, thinking of nothing else throughout the whole race.

Landy had always run his best races from the front. My only worry was that at the last minute he might try to run a waiting race. If he did this, then either of us might win, and the final time would be slow. The race would give no satisfaction either to us or to the spectators. To dissuade him from running this kind of race I tried to demonstrate in the A.A.A. Championships on 10th July 1954, only three weeks before the Empire Games, what might happen if he failed to set a fast enough pace.

I waited behind the field until the beginning of the back straight, 300 yards from the tape. Then I tore home with the fastest sprint I could produce. My time was 4 min. 7.6 sec., and I ran the last lap in 53.8 seconds, almost as fast as I can run a flat 440 yards. I had some added verve for the race because I had qualified as a doctor the day before. Including my research in Oxford, I had been studying and running for nearly eight years.

I knew that the only weak spot in John Landy's racing armoury was his finish, and I now hoped I had convinced him that he must lead. The day before I left for Vancouver I had a long talk with Franz Stampfl. I knew exactly the type of programme that suited me, and so I did not need to see him while I was training myself to a peak. But his advice was invaluable in building up my mental approach to the race. I could carry myself almost all the way. Then at the last minute, when I became hesitant, he helped to give me the confidence and aggressiveness that I previously lacked.

I cast my mind back to the moment of doubt before the four-minute mile. He had reassured me then and all had been well. I had risen to the occasion and had been able to unleash just that extra energy needed to overcome the adverse wind. He convinced me that I could tap this source of energy again. Neither of us underestimated John Landy. He was the greatest miler in the world, both in the consistency of his performances and in the times he had set up. If my mental approach was

227

correct I could beat him. I might only win by inches, but somehow I would win. Landy was stronger and tougher than I, but I felt I could prepare myself better for the great occasion.

The things a man learns for himself he never forgets, and can adapt to many different situations. The things a man does by himself, he does best. Franz Stampfl's greatness as a coach rests on his adaptability and patience. He watches and waits for the moment when the athlete really needs him. Franz once told me of setting a group of young boys the task of traversing a beam suspended above the floor. Some swung along with their hands, some walked upright, some crawled, but none of them fell off. In each method there was some peculiar grace derived from the boy's inventiveness. It would have been possible to show them how to cross the beam correctly. Some would have managed it easily, others would have stifled their natural inclination to do it differently, and might have come to grief.

I think it is the duty of the coach to encourage resource and initiative in each one of us. We do not want to become identical human beings, the servants of a new totalitarianism. We seek individual freedom in a world that of necessity imposes more and more restrictions. The less we can find freedom in our work the more we shall need to find freedom in the games we play.

The aim of the athletic coach should not merely be to

help his pupil to achieve a set performance in his event, to throw the discus 150 feet or to run a mile in 4 min. 10 sec. It should also be to show how, through experiencing the stress imposed by his event, he can understand and master his own personality.

Geoffrey Dyson, the chief A.A.A. coach, has said that he does not believe that a coach can or should alter the mental approach of an athlete towards his event. With respect, I feel this is fundamentally wrong, especially as far as running is concerned. A man's temperament and character can be transformed by the freedom he gains as the result of the correct mental approach.

I sometimes think that running has given me a glimpse of the greatest freedom a man can ever know, because it results in the simultaneous liberation of both body and mind. The mental approach is all important, because the strength and power of the mind are without limit. All this energy can be harnessed by the correct attitude of mind.

Running is creative. The runner does not know how or why he runs. He only knows that he must run, and in so doing he expresses himself as he can in no other way. He creates out of instability and conflict something that gives pleasure to himself and others, because it releases feelings of beauty and power latent within us all. I believe that we must all find some creative activity in which we can achieve a measure of success.

It is not necessary or desirable to have an intellectual

attitude towards running. Of the great runners I have known few could explain the satisfaction they derived from running. This did not detract from their greatness. Indeed it probably added to it. They have almost all been men in whom one could detect great power which had achieved its fullest expression through running. If they had been able to express as effectively the power within themselves in other ways, they would never have needed to run.

For the last year or so the fascination of understanding why athletes run has tended to overshadow my interest in even my own running.

A great welcome awaited the British team in Vancouver. The Canadians were extremely hospitable. British Columbia seems to take its standard of living more from the United States, though it remains pleasantly free from their hurry and bustle. There was a spontaneous and moving speech by the Pakistan captain at the flag-raising ceremony in the Empire Games village.

Soon after our arrival we were invited to go swimming. Driving past the University track we saw Landy training hard. I seized on the chance to get our first meeting over. I should have been embarrassed alone, and I was grateful that Chris Chataway, who had met Landy recently, was with me.

I had not seen Landy for two years, when we ran in the same heat in the Olympic Games, though for the last few months he had never been far from my thoughts. I was conscious of blushing as we met, but he showed no trace of awkwardness. He faced me bare-chested, wearing only running shorts. His dark curly hair was cut short and his tough body bronzed by the sun. He had been running barefoot on the grass between harder bursts on the cinder track. He had a most attractive personality and seemed most friendly. He went on with his training. We went swimming instead, and it may have been on one of these expeditions that I caught my cold.

The glare of publicity over the Empire Games Mile was harsher than ever. Landy and I were the only two runners to have broken the four-minute mile, and we were both at the peak of our training. There had never been a race like this. For some weeks before, journalists had been flying between Scandinavia and England, comparing our chest measurements as if we were professional prize fighters, and trying to find out what toothpaste we used.

The outcome would be final, everyone knew that. The race would settle our rivalry. Chris Chataway, who shared a room with me, was an immense comfort in my anxiety. His confidence in himself and his apparent casualness in training were a steadying influence. His own race in Vancouver meant a great deal to him. His main rival was Freddie Green, also from England, who had beaten him by inches in the A.A.A. three miles championship in which they shared a new world record.

I was glad too that Chris Brasher had been selected for the mile—there was no steeplechase event. A car had been lent to me and together we managed to escape from the "third" eyes of camera men and the irritating pens of gossip writers.

John Landy did all his training on the main track and often had two sessions a day. Details appeared in the newspapers, and very disturbing reading it was for me. On one occasion he ran a 4 min. 13 sec. mile just to warm up, and followed it with a ¾-mile in 2 min. 39 sec. He appeared to have an insatiable appetite for interval running. Before I arrived he had run ten quarter-miles each in 58 seconds, with a 1½ minute recovery interval between each. He confided to me that he thought this was too strenuous!

It was incomparably superior to the best I had ever done—ten quarters in sixty seconds each with a full two minutes interval between each. He ran twice as many 220-yard dashes as I could manage, and in an average time several seconds faster. Until this time I had no first-hand experience of the "hard work" school of training. It made my own preparation seem most inadequate. When I felt depressed, however, I reminded myself that my training had been good enough to run a four-minute mile when conditions were far from ideal, and was content to leave it at that.

The great contrast in our training methods was not lost on the Press. They never saw me running on a track and wondered whether I ever trained at all. One day they noticed an athlete in the British Team, Peter Fryer, running extremely fast on the track. In build and height he looked remarkably like me. Being a sprinter, he was able to run a series of 220-yard dashes at what would have been an astonishing speed for a miler. When I opened my paper next day I was most gratified to read of the improvement in my powers of sprinting! For a minute I hoped that my great rival had taken time off to read the paper too.

Then I thought again. I wanted Landy to remain quite confident until the last minute. As his times were faster than mine he was automatically favourite, and with his splendid public training performances the odds on his winning increased daily. This did not disturb me —I do not regard being favourite as an enviable position.

Was I doing any training at all? With great effort I had run a ¾-mile in 3 min. 1 sec., the day before we left England, and was mainly resting for the final struggle. In Vancouver I did most of my running on a golf course near the University of British Columbia where we were staying. One member of our team was nearly knocked out by a golf ball, but I gladly accepted this small natural hazard in return for the delight of running on soft springy turf away from the crowds. I trained out of the heat of the day when the sun cast long shadows from the pine trees lining the fairways.

My cold grew gradually worse. Why did I have to

catch my first cold of the year the week before I raced against Landy? At my best I stood a chance of beating him, but this cold, now on my chest, seemed to rob me of that chance. Landy would surely waltz away from me. I felt most depressed and dosed myself with all the medicines I could find.

There was one day of training which satisfied me. Chris Chataway and I found a quiet track and were running quarter miles in 60 seconds. Before the last one he suggested that I should lead for the first 220 yards in 31 seconds, and then he would sprint past me at exactly the place where he intended to take the lead in his own race. He would run his fastest.

I said I would hang on and try to overtake him again at the beginning of the final straight. This was the point where I was hoping to wrest the lead from Landy. Chris overtook me as planned, and despite a hard day's training I found I had enough speed left to shoot past him before the finish. Our time for the last 220 yards was 25 seconds. It was a good speed, and I felt well prepared.

In my last training on the Sunday before the race, when my cold was getting worse, I ran a 1 min. 54.7 sec. half-mile. But Landy had run three successive half-miles two days previously in almost as fast a time, so I felt dejected again. I wrapped myself up and waited anxiously for the preliminary heat on the following Thursday.

The preponderance of athletes from the British Isles

234

made the final result of the competition in terms of countries rather a foregone conclusion, and so the events were struggles between individual athletes rather than representative matches. We felt that if a Canadian did not win an event the spectators would next prefer an athlete from the mother country. Very few problems arise at an Empire and Commonwealth meeting where almost every competitor speaks the same language. The incidents that do occur are more often the result of over-excitement among the competitors than of any ill feeling between their countries.

Chris Chataway's convincing victory in the Three Miles was an encouraging omen for my race. It was a wonderful season for Chris. He helped to set up two world records for the mile, mine and Landy's, and himself missed the two-mile record by a fraction of a second. At the White City he established a new world's best time for three miles, but had to share it with the victor in that race, Freddie Green.

As he broke the tape at Vancouver, Chris could feel that his day had come, and a broad grin spread across his face. Chris enjoys all racing tremendously, but like the rest of us, he enjoys it even more when he wins. His defeat at Helsinki in 1952 had cast a shadow on my own performance there. Now I hoped that I could follow him in his good fortune at Vancouver.

There were two heats for the mile on Thursday, with one day's rest before the Final on the Saturday. I still

235

had a thick cold and was worried that I might have a burst of coughing during the race. In my heat Geoffrey Warren, the Australian second string, led with a 59 sec. first quarter. I assumed that he was trying to tempt me into running a four-minute mile, and so tire myself for the struggle in the Final with Landy. He passed the half-mile in two minutes, twenty yards ahead of me. Soon after he dropped out. He looked quite surprised when he saw that I had not been following him. This incident is typical of the unexpected element in races, and of the need to be constantly on the alert. I might easily have been led astray into trying to keep up with Landy's countryman, but I realised in time that his pace was unnecessarily fast.

The final time of my heat, won by Murray Halberg of New Zealand, was 4 min. 7.4 sec., a Games record. I came third in 4 min. 8.4 sec. In the other heat William Baillie of New Zealand came first in 4 min. 11.4 sec., John Landy being third in the same time. Ian Boyd and Chris Brasher came fourth and sixth.

It encouraged me that I could run a mile in 4 min. 8.4 sec. so easily with a bad cold. After all, a good sweat, as everyone knows, is either a kill or cure for a cold, and Empire Games heats may be as good a way as any of achieving a cure. The next day my cold was getting distinctly better and I was regaining the hopeful attitude I had when I arrived in Vancouver.

I am certain that one's feelings at the last minute

236

before a race matter most. Confidence that has been supreme until that moment can be lost quite suddenly. Twice a day I took longish walks, sometimes with Chris Chataway, but often alone. I screwed up my determination to win. Almost for the first time in my life I could say the day before the race that I was really looking forward to it.

There were eight finalists. Apart from John Landy, who was now 4 : 1 favourite, the next best runner was thought to be Murray Halberg, the young New-Zealander, who had run a 4 min. 4 sec. mile at the age of nineteen. He had won my heat but was not as yet very experienced in this class of competition. Bill Ferguson of Canada, now twenty-two, had run a nine-minute two miles, also at the age of nineteen, and earlier in the week had run a 1 min. 52.7 sec. half-mile. Landy was the only Australian left in the Final. David Law and Ian Boyd, both Oxford milers, had also qualified for the Final, and I felt fortunate to have their company.

There were rumours that Murray Halberg might set the pace for Landy for a couple of laps, but I did not take them seriously. I still believed that Landy himself would try to run me off my feet. With Law and Boyd I considered the possibility of going into the lead to restrain him a little and to prevent the total time from being less than four minutes. If it was any faster than this I could not expect to have any finish left. We decided to wait and see what happened.

237

I also had to consider how great a lead I could allow Landy to establish. There were times when he had misjudged the pace and run a first lap in 56 seconds. If he were to do this and I could keep back to 59 seconds, he would play into my hands. By running evenly I might have a greater reserve left at the finish.

On the day of the Final, Saturday 7th August, the stadium was filled with one of the most enthusiastic crowds I have ever seen. The setting was perfect. The newly-built stadium lay there in the sunshine, the flags of the competing countries silhouetted against the mountains of Vancouver Island.

We lined up for the start. Landy was on the inside. The gun fired and Baillie of New Zealand went straight into the lead. I stayed some yards back at Landy's shoulder until he took over the lead at the 220-yard mark. Gradually he drew away, and I lay second at the end of the first lap in 59.2 sec. Landy's pace was too fast for me (58.2 sec.), and I had allowed a gap of seven yards to open up. In the second lap this lead increased at one time to fifteen yards. I completed the half-mile in 1 min. 59 seconds, so I was within a four-minute mile schedule!

By now I had almost lost contact with Landy. I no longer had the advantage of being pulled along by him. The field had split. Landy was out in front on his own and I was leading the rest, ten yards farther back. I felt complete detachment, and at the half-mile remember

238

saying to myself—only two minutes more. The stage was set for relaxed running until my final burst.

My speed was now the same as Landy's. The only problem was that Landy was· a long way in front and looked like staying there. I was on schedule, but he was not slowing down as I had expected. This was the moment when my confidence wavered. Was he going to break the world record again?

To have any "finish" left I must be able to follow at his shoulder throughout the early part of the last lap. How could I close the gap before the bell? If I were to stand any chance of winning I must reach his shoulder before then. I must abandon my own time schedule and run to his. This was the turning point of the race.

I quickened my stride, trying at the same time to keep relaxed. I won back the first yard, then each succeeding yard, until his lead was halved by the time we reached the back straight on the third lap. How I wished I had never allowed him to establish such a lead!

I had now "connected" myself to Landy again, though he was still five yards ahead. I was almost hypnotised by his easy shuffling stride—the most clipped and economical I have ever seen. I tried to imagine myself attached to him by some invisible cord. With each stride I drew the cord tighter and reduced his lead. At the ¾-mile when the bell rang I was at Landy's shoulder. The rest of the field were twenty yards back and I was so absorbed by the man-to-man struggle that I heard no lap time. The real battle was beginning. The two of us were running alone now with all eyes upon us.

The third lap had tired me—my time was 59.6 seconds. This was the lap when a runner expects to slow down a little to gather momentum for the finish, and I had been toiling hard to win back those painful yards. I fixed myself to Landy like a shadow. He must have known I was at his heels because he began to quicken his stride as soon as we turned into the last back straight. It was incredible that in a race run at this speed he should start a finishing burst 300 yards from the tape. I laughed to remember that three weeks before in England I had actually considered whether I might overtake him at the 220-yard mark! Now it was all I could do to hold him.

We passed the 1,500 metres mark in the same time as Landy's world record for that distance, set up during his mile race at Turku in Finland. If Landy did not slacken soon I would be finished. As we entered the last bend I tried to convince myself that he was tiring. With each stride now I attempted to husband a little strength for the moment at the end of the bend when I had decided to pounce. I knew this would be the point where Landy would least expect me, and if I failed to overtake him there the race would be his.

When the moment came my mind would galvanise my body to the greatest effort it had ever known. I knew I was tired. There might be no response, but it was my only chance. This moment had occurred dozens of times

240

before. This time the only difference was that the whole race was being run to my absolute limit.

Just before the end of the last bend I flung myself past Landy. As I did so I saw him glance inwards over his opposite shoulder. This tiny act of his held great significance and gave me confidence. I interpreted it as meaning that he had already made his great effort along the back straight. All round the bend he had been unable to hear me behind him, the noise of the crowd was so great. He must have hoped desperately that I had fallen back. The worry of whether he had succeeded grew on him. His last chance to look round came at the end of the bend. Here, because of the curve of the track, he could see behind him with only half a turn of the head. He knew that to challenge now I must run extra distance, and therefore he did not expect it. The moment he looked round, he was unprotected against me and so lost a valuable fraction of a second in his response to my challenge. It was my tremendous luck that these two happenings—his turning round and my final spurt—came absolutely simultaneously.

In two strides I was past him, with seventy yards to go, but I could not accelerate further. Though I was slowing all the time I just managed to reach the tape, winning by five yards in 3 min. 58.8 sec. Once again the four-minute mile had been broken, this time by both of us in the same race.

This last lap was one of the most intense and exciting

of my life. John Landy had shown me what a race could really be at its greatest. He is the sort of runner I could never become, and for this I admire him. Before Vancouver he achieved a record of solo mile races that I could never have equalled. At Vancouver he had the courage to lead at the same speed in a closely competitive race. His boldness forced me to abandon my time schedule and lose myself quite completely in the struggle itself. After this experience I felt that I could never be interested again in record-breaking without the thrill of competitive struggle.

The crowd was deliriously excited for twenty minutes. Then the joy of triumph suddenly disappeared. All was forgotten as the dazed figure of Jim Peters, in the last stages of exhaustion, appeared at the edge of the stadium. No one who saw the tragic gallantry of his futile attempts to reach the finish wanted the painful exhibition to continue, yet no one seemed to have the authority to remove him from the race.

He crossed the same finishing line as Landy and myself. He did not know his own finish was some 200 yards farther on. One consolation to those who saw the spectacle is that it is unlikely he felt any pain in his grim determination to finish. A second consolation is that neither the sport as a whole nor marathon running in particular should be condemned for this incident, because with greater foresight in planning, it need never have happened.

242

The final placings in the Empire Games Mile were:

|  |  | Min. | Sec. |
|---|---|---|---|
| 1. R. G. Bannister (England) .. | .. | 3 | 58.8 |
| 2. J. Landy (Australia) .. .. | .. | 3 | 59.6 |
| 3. R. Ferguson (Canada) .. | .. | 4 | 4.6 |
| 4. V. Milligan (N. Ireland) .. | .. | 4 | 5.0 |
| 5. M. Halberg (New Zealand).. | .. | 4 | 7.2 |
| 6. I. Boyd (England) .. .. | .. | 4 | 7.2 |
| 7. W. Baillie (New Zealand) .. | .. | 4 | 11.0 |

D. C. Law (England) retired, having lost a shoe.

# CHAPTER SIXTEEN

# CONCLUSION

*"We run because we like it*
*Through the broad bright land."*
SORLEY.

WHEN I STARTED SERIOUS RUNNING eight years ago I was seeking an outlet for something I did not understand which could not be expressed in any other way. The incentive to my running was part of a strange conflict—similar I suppose to the conflicts which exist in all of us. This was coupled with the desire to prove my ability to do something well. I set out to do it alone.

Sooner or later in sport we run into situations that are too big for us to master. In real life we can dodge them. We can play hide and seek with reality, never facing the truth about ourselves. In sport we cannot. It shakes our roots with its confusing pattern of success and failure. As a result, sport leads to the most remarkable self-discovery—of our limitations as well as of our abilities. The discovery is partly physical; one learns for example that feeling tired does not mean that the limit of exhaustion has been reached. But mainly the discovery is mental, brought about by the stresses that sport imposes.

Self-discovery is most rapid if we set out on the early stages alone. I soon learnt how far from being self-sufficient I was, and realised the value of the co-operation and assistance of others. But unless I had gone as far as possible alone, I should never have known the questions other people could best answer for me and those I must answer for myself. Ten years ago, in the confusion of growing up, it seemed so hard to achieve a personal sense of freedom. It still seems difficult, but I know now that the struggle is worth while.

To me, action has never come easily. We can allow ourselves to be blown along like leaves in a storm, or we can try to take action. We live in a world of uncertainties, but there comes a moment when we are called to face the starting pistol. The strain connected with sport has helped me to bear this burden of uncertainty.

We all have ideals, and as we grow up we have the choice whether to pursue or to give them up. If we pursue them we may not attain them. At times we may wonder whether there is any point in the pursuit, because of the sacrifices involved. We can see so many ideals, so why concentrate on one? There are so many temptations to remain a dilettante. Life consists partly in the tempering of ideals, to bring the finishing tape nearer, partly in a continual and restless reaching towards it.

Adolescence is a time of conflict and bewilderment. When we are not master in our own house, how can we expect to be at ease and happy in our relations with other people? Perhaps these years can be weathered

245

more successfully if we develop some demanding activity
that tests to the limit our bodies as well as our minds.
We can then start from the point of discovering how
much our bodies can endure before they crack—in most
cases a great deal more than we should have guessed.
This discovery may encourage us to greater efforts in the
mental field.

Each of us has to find this activity for himself. It may
be mountain climbing, running or sailing, or it may be
something quite different. The important thing is that
we should perform ourselves rather than watch others.
By absorption in the pursuit we forget ourselves and it
fills the void between the child and the man. Later when
we find our career or other loves, we are surprised at the
extent to which we have grown. By then we are no
longer in a position to make the sacrifices we formerly
hardly noticed.

The activity we choose should, I think, become a
striving to achieve more and more, not for purely selfish
motives, but because of the recognition of some higher
purpose. The aim is to move with the greatest possible
freedom towards the realisation of the best within us.
This is the quest of a lifetime, and sport plays only a
small part in it.

It is only while we are young that the unquiet pulse
of our mind poses so many questions, is restless to experience, and refuses to take the easy way out. The
chance comes only once. These doubts cannot be tackled from the arm-chair. To do so produces an obsession

of self-analysis which is unhealthy. Yet these very doubts can inspire our practical endeavours, as in sport, or our striving to achieve something that has not been accomplished before. No one has exhausted the possibilities that arise from harnessing this uncertainty. This is one reason why I think it foolhardy to predict the absolute limits of human endeavour.

The last few years have covered a strange period in the history of athletics. They have seen the introduction of a new professionalism, not in the sense of unlimited financial reward, but in devoting unlimited time and energy to sport. Every country is seeking to enhance national prestige through physical achievements. It may be in establishing new jet-plane speed or altitude records, penetrating the depths of the sea, or scaling the world's highest mountains. Too few questions are asked about the means, provided the end of national glory is achieved.

I have tried to show that running refuses to fit into a pattern of this kind. If more and more work and time will bring about improvement in performance, then studies and vocations will not be allowed to stand in the way. Two years ago I felt depressed at this thought. If Zatopek ran sixty quarter miles in sixty seconds each, in a single work-out, it seemed that only a man who could train still harder could beat him. Where would it all end?

Running would have lost its purpose. But this has not happened. I believe, and I know there are other runners who agree, that running has proved to be a truly

247

amateur activity after all, on which it is neither necessary nor desirable to spend unlimited time and energy. Fitting running into the rest of life until one's work becomes too demanding—this is the burden and joy of the true amateur. Running is more than just slogging at training. Excessive training quickens the rate of recovery, but it has yet to be shown that performance is better on the day of the race.

I have tried to describe my individual conception of running. What place has this in a world in which sport has become a matter of great importance for national prestige? How can sport be prevented from becoming infected with the differences that exist between countries in the political sphere?

We must, I think, realise that countries will organise their sport in different ways—it is a matter of national temperament, like the political party men follow, or the newspaper they read. We must leave the choice to them. Some countries will prefer a system of incentives that we should regard as almost professional, but this does not detract from the simplicity and purity of the ideals of the individual athlete. If we can continue international competition in sport on an ever-increasing scale with this in mind, athletes, and through them, spectators, will be drawn to a closer understanding of these very differences of temperament.

I am sure that athletics will safeguard itself, and for this reason, that it has essentially an individual not a national basis. We run, not because we think it is doing us good, but because we enjoy it and cannot help ourselves. It also does us good because it helps us to do other things better. It gives a man or woman the chance to bring out power that might otherwise remain locked away inside. The urge to struggle lies latent in everyone. The more restricted our society and work become, the more necessary it will be to find some outlet for this craving for freedom. No one can say, "You must not run faster than this, or jump higher than that." The human spirit is indomitable.

# THE EVOLUTION OF
# THE MILE RECORD

## My Steps To The First Four-Minute Mile

**1946**

October—Freshmen's Sports, Oxford                    4:53.0

**1947**

March 22nd—Oxford v. Cambridge, White City           4:30.8
June 5th—A.A.A. v. Oxford, Oxford                     4:24.6

**1948**

March 20th—Oxford v. Cambridge, White City           4:23.4
May 6th—A.A.A. v. Oxford, Oxford                      4:22.8
June 19th—Kinnaird Trophy Meeting, Chiswick          4:18.7
July 3rd—A.A.A. Championships, White City            4:17.2

**1949**

March 12th—Oxford v. Cambridge, White City           4:16.2
June 11th—Oxford and Cambridge v. Cornell and
       Princeton in U.S.A.                            4:11.1

1950
Dec. 30th—Centennial Games, New Zealand     4:9.9

1951
April 28th—Benjamin Franklin Mile, Philadelphia     4:8.3
July 14th—A.A.A. Championships, White City     4:7.8

1953
May 2nd—A.A.A. v. Oxford, Oxford     4:3.6
June 27th—Motspur Park     4:2.0

1954
May 6th—A.A.A. v. Oxford, Oxford     3:59.4
August 7th—British Empire Games, Vancouver     3:58.8

# The Mile Record Since My Retirement From Running

1954
John Landy, Australia     3:58.0

1957
Derek Ibbotson, England     3:57.2

1958
Herb Elliott, Australia     3:54.5

1962
Peter Snell, New Zealand                              3:54.4

1964
Peter Snell, New Zealand                              3:54.1

1965
Michel Jazy, France                                   3:53.6

1966
Jim Ryun, United States                               3:51.3

1967
Jim Ryun, United States                               3:51.1

1975
Filbert Bayi, Tanzania                                3:51.0
John Walker, New Zealand                              3:49.4

1979
Sebastian Coe, England                                3:49.0

1980
Steve Ovett, England                                  3:48.8

1981
Sebastian Coe, England                                3:48:5
Steve Ovett, England                                  3:48:4
Sebastian Coe, England                                3:47:3

1985
Steve Cram, England                                   3:46:3